In this refreshing, well researched, mind-stretching study, Joe Barnard challenges men to ask the bigger questions of life, have the courage to analyse their own hearts, and embark on a life shaping journey, via Plato's cave, to Jesus Christ. Highly recommended.

Jeremy McQuoid
Pastor, Deeside Christian Fellowship Church, Aberdeen
Chair of Trustees, Keswick Ministries

In *The Road Back to God*, Joe Barnard gives us a prequel to his helpful men's discipleship book, *The Way Forward*. Taking note of the current cultural trend which includes an increased openness amongst men to Christianity, Joe has written an excellent introduction to the gospel and a real challenge to men. It is an unusually helpful evangelistic book – and a lovely refresher for those who are already Christians. I look forward to using it in a men's study group

David Robertson
Minister, Scots Kirk, Newcastle, Australia

In the past Joe Barnard has thought very deeply about Christian men and written so helpfully for them. His latest book, *The Road Back to God*, is another triumph in seeking to turn men towards Christ. In light of a recent uptick in curiosity from men about Jesus, he is clear from the start that this is not for every man but for the man with a flicker of interest in Christianity. Which makes it a unique read. Then he guides his reader, from the position he is in now to the destination of gospel transformation. Each chapter builds on the one before and like a good coach he encourages and directs along the way, dealing with the big questions of life, the big problems of life and the solution to it all. I think perhaps the greatest commendation I could give this book is that as I was reading I just kept thinking of the amount of men I know who would benefit from it. Take up and read!

Gavin Peacock
Pastor, Bethersden Baptist Church, UK

With precision and clarity, Joe puts his finger right on the pulse of what so many men—young and old—are feeling and experiencing about their place and purpose, given our cultural moment. With refreshing and accessible insight as well as a firm grasp on theology, philosophy, sociology, and ethics, like a sk

our defences and lays down the gauntlet. Issuing the challenge to any man who cares to ask the big questions of life and the pursuit of truth, this book will dare you to wrestle with ancient wisdom; to step out on the road of faith and holiness; and to come have a closer look at the person of Jesus Christ.

Steve Osmond
Speaker and writer
Solas Centre for Public Christianity, UK

Many men today find themselves deeply dissatisfied with the world they inhabit. Disappointed by the emptiness of secularism, bruised by the legacy of feminism, and increasingly skeptical of a morally bankrupt culture, the quest for a reality beyond the merely material is fuelling an awakening in spirituality. However, much mainstream Christianity has imbibed the corruption of the culture around, which is the very thing men are rejecting. Thinking men are seeking truth, and want to know what authentic Christianity really is. Joe Barnard has set out to help, by guiding your steps to find honest answers in the original Scriptures, the foundation of the orthodox faith. Let him lead you there, where the real Jesus Christ may be encountered, and his ultimate truth revealed.

William J. U. Philip
Senior Minister, The Tron Church, Glasgow

Men feel adrift. Worse, we've gladly turned to the popular diviners of meaning—tell-it-like-it-is public intellectuals like Jordan Peterson, or even Joe Rogan. *The Road Back to God* offers a more incisive view of our lethargic unease, offering the good news of Jesus and the intellectual world of Scripture as a way to see ourselves and the universe more truly. Joe Barnard, yet again, speaks plainly and holds out a hand to lift us from narrow and anxiety-driven views in the foxhole. He raises us up to stand on the hill and survey what God can do with us. Give this book to any young (or old) man that just wants a map back to God.

Dru Johnson
Director, Abrahamic Theistic Origins Project, Wycliffe Hall, Oxford; Templeton Senior Research Fellow

THE ROAD BACK TO GOD

FAITH FOR MEN
DISSATISFIED BY
THE MODERN WORLD

JOE BARNARD

CHRISTIAN
FOCUS

print ISBN 978-1-5271-1272-8
ebook ISBN 978-1-5271-1370-1

10 9 8 7 6 5 4 3 2 1

Published in 2025
Christian Focus Publications Ltd,
Geanies House, Fearn, Ross-shire,
IV20 1TW, Scotland.

www.christianfocus.com

Cover design by James Amour

Printed and bound by Bell & Bain, Glasgow

MIX
Paper | Supporting
responsible forestry
FSC
www.fsc.org
FSC® C007785

I dedicate this book to

David Lyle Jeffrey

*whose footnotes have been the footprints that I've
followed in faith seeking understanding.*

Contents

The Rise of Religious Interest Among Men

Something weird has happened in recent years. Modern men are finding themselves strangely interested in Christianity. In restaurants and bars, a droll question is being repeated with increasing seriousness: "What if the crazy Christians are right?"

I feel confident in saying that very few experts anticipated this trend. Whether looking at large-scale trajectories since the Enlightenment or listening to the shrill barking of the new atheists of the early 2000s, most critics have assumed that Christianity was taking a last gasp before giving up the ghost. Yet, like Jesus Himself, Christianity seems to have the propensity to resurrect as soon as it dies. No matter how vigorously tyrants and philosophers try to seal the cave and bury the body, the stone always ends up rolled away and news spreading that there is more to Jesus than meets the eye.

And thus it seems that a lot of men today find themselves unexpectedly curious about the faith of their forefathers. They may not yet believe in Jesus, but they respect Him and want to learn more about Him. They have the niggling feeling that somewhere tucked away under the floorboards of Western civilization is a dusty Bible and an old, wooden cross. In fact, the suspicion is even greater: men are wondering whether these old relics might not just be the pillars holding up the moral fabric of the modern world – at least the part of it that is worth conserving.[1]

But, flirting with Christianity is one thing; becoming an actual Christian is something else. The interest of a lot of guys might be compared to seeing an attractive girl on the opposite side of the street. They admire from a distance; however, walking over and making a connection is a step they are hesitant to take. In the present moment, men are open to thinking about principles of traditional morality or about how the demise of Christendom may account for the social decay of the world around them. But here they stop and sit comfortably on the fence. In most cases, men are not finding their way into churches, and they are not staying up late at night reading a Bible. Instead, like teenage boys feeling a first crush, they are admiring Christianity from afar without understanding much about what is attracting them.

In many ways, such reluctance is not surprising. Men today are distanced from Jesus not just by time but by multiple layers of culture. To pick up on a famous image, there often appears to be a broad and ugly ditch separating the modern world and the truth claims of the New Testament. This can leave a man feeling as if he is looking at Jesus from afar through a telescope, but uncertain of how to bridge the abyss so that Jesus and he are standing on the same soil. A man looks out of his window and sees paved roads,

---

1. David Brooks, Douglas Murray, Tom Holland, Jordan Peterson, and Russell Brand are all intelligent, popular voices that have stirred renewed interest in Christianity among men. There is also a growing number of "cultural Christians," a list which includes Elon Musk, Peter Thiel, and, strangely, even Richard Dawkins.

plasma screens, fancy gadgets, and busy commerce. He then picks up a Bible and reads about priests, sin, blood rituals, and crucifixion. The first set of items is incontestably real, tangible, and important. The second feels foreign, detached, and of little consequence. Therefore, for a lot of guys, Jesus is something like a cloud – an object nice to look at for a minute or two, but utterly disconnected from the turf where the game of life is actually played.[2]

This distance between Jesus and modern life can leave a man with little motivation to go out and investigate what it means to be a Christian. Sure, he might listen in to a spiritual conversation if an internet celebrity like Bishop Barron is featured on Jordan Peterson's podcast. However, such interest is, at most, casual. When it comes to the business of a normal day, working through questions about the resurrection of Jesus is located on the to-do list just beneath "brush up on Spanish" and "learn the bass guitar," Most men live by the assumption that a good and successful life does not require any nailed-down religious convictions. Wealth creation, life management, health and fitness – even politics and sports – these are the topics that matter on a Thursday afternoon. The fine points of God, ethics, and salvation are like bar nuts at a pub counter: one can take them or leave them according to appetite.

And yet, this lukewarmness of interest does not cancel the remarkable phenomenon that is happening on both sides of the Atlantic. The amazing thing about the present moment is not that a lot of men are minimally concerned about religious topics; historically, that is the norm. What is surprising is that there is a spiritual ember in the hearts of

---

2. Tom Wright has diligently worked to explain the history behind this gap and to dismantle it. See N.T. Wright, *History and Eschatology* (SPCK, 2019).

swathes of men that did not exist ten years ago.[3] Even if the curiosity amounts to little more than a bare coal, it is there and glowing. There is something about the modern world that for the first time in decades – in some cases centuries – is stirring the ashes of faith. Guys dotted across the Western world are warming to faith rather than cooling. This is something most pundits did not see coming.

Now, this book is a guide for men who feel themselves drifting in the direction of the Christian faith. The word "guide" is worth pausing to reflect on. Often, guide-books are resources that offer a general overview of a subject to people with no prior knowledge on the topic. Thus, if one sees a "guide to Italian cooking," he might assume that the book provides a user-friendly summary of the common recipes and practices that go into making Italian food. In line with this, a man might pick up this book thinking that it will be something like an extended encyclopedia entry outlining the common beliefs and practices of Christians – of one variety or another. This is *not* the case. Few men have the stamina needed to finish any encyclopedia entry, much less an extended one!

A different kind of "guide" is what a person might purchase if he is about to take a trek through the Grand Canyon. The goal of such a book is not a general overview, but a safe and successful passage. Such a guide will carefully curate information according to the criteria of what is useful and necessary to prepare for, undertake, and complete the journey from start to finish. More than likely, such a book will create a sense of movement and pace. There will be a way in which the structure of the book itself will map out

---

3. Who would have imagined a decade or two ago that there would be millions of men on YouTube watching academic lectures on Old Testament books by someone like Jordan Peterson?

an itinerary that is meant to be put to use by the reader as he ventures forth, plodding his way into the wild.

This sense of offering an itinerary captures the essence of this book. It is written with the expectation that the average man will be starting from a common "location" and needing guidance to progress toward a targeted "destination." The starting point is what might be labeled a secular identity. Men are not just inhabitants of the modern world; they have unconsciously put on a modern mode of being. In other words, they are caught up in patterns of belief and behavior which distance them from being able to understand and embody a very different way of life. It's this gap between a secular existence and a Christian existence that creates the need for a book that is not just an overview, but an itinerary. Men need a guide that does more than merely explain what Christianity is – as if the religion were some dusty artifact in the back room of a museum. They need someone to dress them up in what the New Testament refers to as the "gospel" so that, perhaps for the first time ever, they can feel what it's like to live in a world in which holiness and sin are as real and impactful as gravity and light.

If this sounds confusing, a different way of thinking about the needs of modern men is this: Men are not starting from a position of neutrality. They are not blank slates that just need Christian doctrines to be inscribed on them. Instead, there is a kind of deficit that results from participating in a spiritually decadent culture. To move toward faith, two things are therefore required. Men must be unschooled of certain beliefs and practices while, at the same time, being re-schooled in what amounts to something closer to a form of life than a mere set of beliefs. The aim of this book is to guide men through this deep transformation.

Now, it's important to be exceedingly clear about who will benefit from this book – and who will *not*. First, this book is not for committed atheists. There are numerous books written by very bright Christians that take up the trench lines dug by amateur philosophers and combat them. The end result of such bombardment tends to be a stalemate. Skepticism, if entrenched, only burrows more deeply when assaulted. The reason for this is not difficult to grasp. If the pursuit of truth is imagined to be a battlefield with pre-established positions, there is little openness to fresh perspective. The opposing voice is perceived to be a threat, not an asset. Thus, everyone ends up protecting a heavily fortified citadel rather than locking arms on a common quest.

Second, this book is not for men whose religious interests are only roused by the sight of the most recent flag hoisted by the culture wars. A person can no more discover wisdom by thinking at the level of the headlines than he can explore the ocean by standing at the shoreline. Real encounters with truth require something more immersive than splashing in the foam of whatever washes up on social media. If men are looking for a book to justify political anger or social disgust, this is not it. This book is about discerning truth, not fomenting what Nietchze dubbed *ressentiment*. Such discernment always requires diving beneath the spume of "issues" and "topics" in order to see things from the depths of submerged principles. Our challenge throughout the book will be to swim deep enough to appreciate broad currents of thought without plunging so deep that we end up being drowned in the fathomless trenches of academic discussions.

So, what kind of man will benefit from this book? The answer is anyone who has a flicker of interest in Christianity and who is willing to undertake what amounts to an intellectual pilgrimage of faith. The two entry requirements for pressing on are nothing more than a curious mind and a willingness to second-guess the habits of a secular heart. If you can tick these boxes, then *tolle lege*, take up and read.

There is one last thing to be said by way of introduction. The itinerary outlined is going to begin at an unusual point of departure. One would suspect that a journey of faith would start with overtly religious questions or topics. Thus, for example, one might think that the first rule of belief would be something like figuring out the meaning of the word "god." Yet, as was alluded to earlier, men are not just needing to journey toward faith, they are needing to exit out of what constitutes a modern identity, even more specifically, a modern *male* identity. One implication of this is that the barriers to faith are not restricted to the intellect. It's not just that doubts and questions need to be overcome; apathy and indifference also need to be overcome. It's not just that truth needs to be understood; in some cases, truth also needs to be felt. It's not just that men need to figure out what they believe; a lot of men need first to be prompted to think. All of this means that the journey to faith starts much further back than might be expected. We can't get to the foothills of religion until we first find a way out of the spiritual malaise that is endemic among men raised in the backwaters of therapeutic consumerism.

A final word before the journey begins: Christians often refer to Abraham as the father of faith. There is a passage about Abraham in the letter to the Hebrews that says, "And he went out, not knowing where he was going." This remark should comfort you at the outset of this book. If the great Abraham started his spiritual itinerary in a state of confusion, we should not be surprised if we begin in a similar condition. When it comes to the quest for truth, our launch point is of little significance. What matters is that we listen for the voice of wisdom and, once that voice is heard, that we follow her trail like hounds on the hunt.

There are two kinds of people one can call reasonable; those who serve God with all their heart because they know Him, and those who seek Him with all their heart because they do not know Him.

—Pascal

Ask Bigger Questions

Men like to think of themselves as self-sufficient and powerful. If we were to pick an animal for an avatar, a lot of us would look for something big and strong. We admire the poise of a lion, the suave of a jaguar, and the independence of a bear. Yet, most men have little in common with the creatures that they respect. A more honest set of symbols to render the character of a typical man would be something like a sheep or a goat – animals that represent a herd instinct rather than a fierce and indomitable will. Although the truth may be painful to hear, human beings are not, by nature, independent and autonomous creatures. The vast majority of us prefer the safety, comfort, and ease of following a crowd to being burdened by the responsibility and risk of needing to blaze a new trail or map an unknown territory.

Why is this? A part of the answer, no doubt, comes from the aversion we feel toward being isolated. It's interesting the degree to which modern people are agitated by solitude. It only takes a few minutes in a quiet home or car before we feel an itch to turn on a screen or listen to music. There is something soothing about the anonymous voice of a talking stranger; such noise buffers us from the discomfort of being isolated in a room with nothing to do but listen to the ramblings of an introspective mind.[1]

Yet, although we feel protected while drifting among the masses, such safety is no more than an aspirin and comfort, a band-aid. In the gospels, there is a disturbing story of a legion of demons asking Jesus to enter a herd of pigs. After Jesus grants the bizarre request, the pigs rush off together toward a nearby cliff, over which they fall and perish en masse. The strange story is a warning to anyone naively trusting in the collective wisdom of a crowd. Following a herd is only safe if the herd is moving in a safe direction. A tranquil march in the direction of a cliff may well, in the end, turn out to be a communal act of suicide.

We ought to feel this danger. Not every culture or society is equally delinquent. Even among the ancient Greeks and Romans, there were high and low tides of moral depravity. Sadly, we are currently living at the front end of what appears to be a nascent Dark Age.[2] This is a moment when we ought to be particularly careful about mindlessly following the tracks of people around us. It's horrifying to think back to a time when people happily used lead paints to decorate children's bedrooms and lead pipes to bring water to their taps. Such blithe stupidity is an emblem for making sense of the cultural moment we are living through. We cannot check our phone, glance at a billboard, or watch a film without consuming some form of spiritual toxin. Although we may no longer

---

1. No one has exposed the spiritual roots of this aversion to solitude more profoundly than Pascal in his *Pensées*.

2. Evidence of this is the near impossibility for contemporary artists to imagine anything other than a dystopian future. Gone is the optimism of modernity. We live in an age that foresees endless technological advancement at the expense of the values and modes of living that make us human.

be stuffing asbestos into our attics, we are insulating our minds with advertisements and messaging which is equally asphyxiating. Such is the risk of a herd mentality in modern times. To graze passively among the crowd in today's world is every bit as hazardous as joining a demon-possessed mob stampeding toward a deadly ridge.[3]

In light of this, the question you need to be asking is this: what does it look like for you today to break free from the herd? Or, to change the metaphor, what does it look like to pull the handbrake on life so that – perhaps for the first time ever – you can get perspective on where you currently are and where you ought to be going?

The answer to this question is surprisingly simple. The first rule of a better life is to start asking questions – and not just more questions, but *better* ones. A good question is like a splash of cold water on a drowsy face. It shocks the nervous system into a more alert and defensive posture. All of us in the modern age need to assume that we are in a stupor. Even if we have not been intentionally imbibing the lies of the culture around us, there are enough fumes in the air to leave us high. Thus, the road to sobriety is the same for everyone. We need to start asking better questions so that we can begin to remap the contours of what is good, true, normal, and real.

This chapter is a crash course for guys new to the sport of thinking. The three questions to be discussed have been chosen due to their special ability to disrupt a herd mentality. To ask any one of them is to dig in the heels and hoist up the chin so that, instead of merely keeping pace with the plodders around us, a strong first step can be taken toward the nobility of thinking for ourselves.

---

3. The image is inspired by a comment in George Grant's *Time as History* (University of Toronto, 1995).

The Question of a Pedestrian:
Where Am I Going?

Imagine that you are standing on the main street of a bustling city center. There are throngs of people heading in every available direction. Your job is randomly to stop people and to ask them one question: *Where are you going?* For an hour you faithfully perform the task at hand and speak to dozens of people.

Now, what do you think would be the end result of such fieldwork? One outcome is nearly certain. Almost everyone interviewed would be able to give an immediate and confident answer to the question. One person would say, "I'm off to work"; another, "I'm picking up the kids from school"; and someone else, "I'm on my way to the bank." The exception to the rule would be anyone needing time to think or who shrugs his shoulders in a gesture of uncertainty. Pedestrians are pedestrians because they are going somewhere. If no destination were in mind, they would still be at home.

Now, let's add a new detail to the imagined scene. You are still randomly stopping people and asking them the same thing. However, the question now refers to a much wider horizon. You are no longer asking people about a physical destination; you are now asking them about an existential destination. You are trying, in other words, to figure out the big purpose, or governing intent, that is guiding their mundane, day-to-day decisions.

We need to realize that a question like *"Where are you going?"* can be understood on multiple levels. Most literally, it just refers to the next location that is on a person's mind (e.g., a grocery store or coffee shop). Yet, figuratively, the question can refer to a "spiritual" condition that a person hopes to attain in the midst of life or achieve at the end of life (e.g., success, fame, wealth, respect, etc.). Human existence is peculiar in that it happens on multiple frequencies at once. We combine material, social, spiritual, and moral objectives into a single life. Thus, in our day-to-day lives, we are not just going in physical directions; we are also following what some philosophers have labeled a "quest."[4] This is true whether we are aware of the fact or not. Beneath the choppy waves of our seemingly disconnected choices is a deep and prevailing spiritual current. All of us are in pursuit of a grand source of significance, purpose, or happiness. Yet, the strange thing is, a lot of us aren't aware of the trajectory of our choices. Rather than being sailboats guided by rudders, we are driftwood caught in the sea.

This in mind, imagine stopping a random person on the street and asking, "Where are you going *in life*?" There is a good chance that, even after sufficient explanation and extra time to think, the person would be silent, even dumbfounded. He would struggle to answer, not because there is no algorithm behind his choices, but because he is not sufficiently self-aware to track the data of his heart.

There is something absurd about how content a lot of men are to float through life. Life is a finite resource of incalculable value. If a child were brought to Disney World and told that he could only take one ride, even a five-year-old would pause and reflect about which one to choose. The choice would feel momentous as he weighed the merits of a Dumbo ride against the thrill of Spinning Teacups. Following the same logic, one would suppose that weathered, competent adults would think carefully before deciding how to use the single-ticket of life. Yet, bizarrely, this is not the case for everyone.

---

4. Two of the best philosophers on the role of "quest" in self-identity are Charles Taylor and Paul Ricoeur. See in particular Ricoeur's *Time and Narrative* trilogy and Taylor's *Sources of the Self* (Harvard University Press, 1992).

It is no exaggeration to say that a lot of men are content to go through life as if they were domesticated animals. They graze on whatever fodder is handed to them, never thinking that there might be greener pastures elsewhere or that, if they paused to look above the grass, they might catch sight of shining stars.[5]

If you are guilty of the tendency to drift through life, now is an opportunity to wake up. A single question can stir the heart out of a living daydream. All you need to do is ask yourself a question that any casual pedestrian can answer, namely, "Where am I going?." As soon as the question is posed, an anchor is released that checks the movement of a free-floating soul. A touch of the dignity of human nature is instantly restored. Instead of passively yielding to the customs of a nameless crowd, you begin to perform one of the most dangerous deeds possible: You begin to think.[6]

The Question of a Sociologist: Who Am I Following?

Let's go back to our imagined fieldwork in a city center. We stop a man and ask him, "Where are you going?" He tells us that he is headed to a local school. We then ask, "Why are you going there?" He says that he is picking up his seven-year-old son. The conversation ends, and he moves on.

Simple decisions, like going to a school to pick up a child, are the product of the human will. The mind is aware of

---

5. Contrasting the natures of animals with the dignity of man, Thomas Watson, a great Puritan theologian, says, "A swine may see an acorn under a tree but he cannot see a star." The quote is found in Watson's invaluable work, *A Body of Divinity* (Reformed Church Publications, 2015).

6. George Orwell warned of "protective stupidity" as a controlled condition for human beings in *1984*. Asking questions is how we break out of such stupidity.

relevant information, and the will determines a course of action based on that information. The process is as straightforward as seeing loose shoelaces and tying them.

Yet, not every choice is so simple.

Imagine that we stop another man on the street. This time the question is not, "Where are you going *right now*?" but, "Where are you going *in life*?" Picture that, after a little reflection, the man is able to identify his deep ambition. He tells us that, more than anything else, he wants to be successful; he longs for the satisfaction of having achieved something of lasting value in a career. Now, keep the scene rolling in your mind. Having heard this (and feeling a bit cheeky), we decide to follow up with a last question. We ask, "Why?" – that is to say, "Why, of all obtainable ends in life, have you identified success as the holy grail of happiness?"

It's intriguing to think about what might happen at this juncture of the conversation. Could a typical man provide a satisfactory reply? It's hard enough for most people to figure out *where* they are going in life; giving cogent reasons for a self-imposed lifestyle is a depth of thinking that a lot of men have never visited.

Indeed, one of the stranger aspects of human behavior is that, while we can give a reason for a lot of immediate actions, when life is viewed from a high point of elevation, we often lose the plot. Each day when we hop in the car to drive to work, we know exactly what we are doing. Yet, when we consistently prioritize career above marriage, or social media above embodied friendship, we are often blind to our choices. In fact, in many cases, we don't even realize that a choice was made at all. We operate more like robots following a pre-set program than spiritual creatures with the god-like faculties of reason and will.[7]

---

7. One of the most insightful, practical, and amusing accounts of

The folly of this self-*un*consciousness is worth pondering. Human beings have an extraordinary tendency to sacrifice their lives on the altar of an unknown god. To pick one example, there are millions of people in the English-speaking world who are as devoted to building a resume as medieval monks were to mortifying the flesh. Yet, unlike the early Franciscans, we moderns have never been through a time of probation in which we discerned a sense of calling. We don't go on a retreat and, after a month of quiet reflection, make the decision that climbing the corporate ladder, or exhausting our youth on gaming, is the most efficient route to happiness. Although a decision is made, it often happens unwittingly. The spiritual software that governs the heart is something that we tend to download and update without understanding much of what is going on. Even if we know "what" we are doing with our lives, we rarely know "why" we are doing it.

This propensity to submit blindly to unidentified values and norms is a massive spiritual liability. Philosophy and history are full of reputable voices warning us that a lot of the most common paths through life end tragically in a barren and joyless wasteland. In fact, while religions and philosophies differ in terms of what they tell us to pursue in life, a surprising number of them are in agreement in terms of what they tell us to avoid. In spite of the allure of pleasure, money, and power, one is hard pressed to find a sage in history who identifies one of these as the endzone of happiness. And yet, take stock of society today. What are the religions that govern the lives of most people? They are not Christianity, Islam, and Hinduism; they are pleasure, money, and power. The spirituality of countless people is a

---

the nonconscious in human behavior is *The Social Animal* by David Brooks (Short Books Limited, 2012)

mad rush in the very direction that the best and wisest of human beings flag as being a cul-de-sac.

There is no excuse for such behavior. Although the herd instinct is strong, it is not indomitable. Human beings are unique in the animal kingdom for their ability to pause and pivot the meaningful direction of their lives. Such countermotion begins with the irksome task of thinking. For novices, this is a two-step process. Step one is figuring out the direction in which you are currently moving. This knowledge constitutes basic self-awareness. Step two is asking, *"Why am I going in this direction?"* This follow-up question is the gear-shift between alertness and autonomy.[8] For as long as we are ignorant of the hidden "why" beneath our actions, we are existing as a mere cipher in a crowd. An unidentified authority is holding the reins of our heart. However, when we begin to test our underlying motives, we wake up to a new degree of moral agency. Instead of blindly acting according to a script, we begin to self-direct.

Now, the following point is exceedingly important. For most guys, the "why" question will be answered, not by looking back to a historical decision, but by looking back to a historical attachment.[9] In other words, for most men, the "why" question will have a "who" answer. Human love is a social contagion. We tend to contract the passions and ideals of the communities within which we are embedded.

---

8. Eventually, some of the dangers associated with autonomy will need to be discussed. However, at this very early stage of moral development, self-direction is a critical step beyond blind conformity.

9. Augustine was the first and most insightful thinker to understand the degree to which human identity is shaped by common objects of love. His *Confessions* is a dramatic picture of the way in which attachments and love go hand-in-hand. See also Oliver O'Donovan, *Common Objects of Love: Moral Reflection and the Shaping of Community* (Eerdmans, 2002).

This is a natural outworking of our herd instinct. We don't just mindlessly follow the footsteps of the society to which we belong; in doing so, we also internalize a scorecard and rulebook that instruct us on how to win in life. Inevitably, we are schooled in a scale of values and a set of rituals that silently but persistently guide us on a path that – in theory at least – is supposed to nudge us toward happiness. In this sense, all of us are living examples of the truthfulness of the old Proverb: "Train up a child in the way he should go and in the end he will not depart from it."

In case there is any confusion on this point, let me illustrate it. Picture a thirty-year-old lawyer in hot pursuit of success. Ask the question, how did he get swept into the current of an unrelenting passion? Although at college he chose a degree program, there was no point at high school or college when he deliberately chose a life-steering passion. The insatiable appetite for achievement was not something that he selected from a shelf after looking at a variety of options; it was something more like a preexisting condition that was present and active even while unseen and unfelt. Where did it come from? The answer will not be uncovered by looking inward, but by looking outward. Multiple decades of competitive sports, merit-based education, and private piano lessons are just a few of the key factors to consider. Having been born into a family and a society that measures worth by accomplishment, this man's career choice is a mere by-product of the culture around him. He may view himself as being independent, decisive, and unique, but the truth is that his actions are no more unusual than a cow grazing in a familiar meadow.

Taking this into consideration, when looking for the big "why" beneath our lifestyles, we need to learn a lesson from sociologists. Sociologists are known for observing the broader movements and trends of a society so that they can understand the actions of an individual. This basic insight – that human beings are more social than we are willing to admit – is a truth that none of us can afford to neglect. Too many guys, if they are given at all to self-reflection, content themselves with the wisdom of life-planning. They think that they can direct their lives by only asking two questions: (a) where do I want to go in life? and (b) how do I get there? Sociology exposes the naivety of such thinking. If we do not take time to inventory the dominant influences around us, our strategic attempts at life-management will be governed by the idols of an invisible tribe. We will end up exhausting our lives in pursuit of a vision that turns out to be nothing more than a mass-marketed template downloaded from mainstream culture (or one of its tributaries). If you are interested in spiritual growth, you need to avoid such foolishness.

The Question of the Philosopher: Is the Altar Worth the Sacrifice?

Earlier an analogy was used of a child being given a ticket for one ride at an amusement park. We need to double-click that scene now and explore its relevance for contemporary men.

Picture the child walking through the park, surveying the rollercoasters, scramblers, drop towers, and bumper cars. Children are not known for being slow and deliberate. The well-known marshmallow experiment is a tell-tale example of how kids typically let impulse govern reason. Nevertheless, here is a child modeling patience and attentiveness. Only after a careful study of all that the park contains does he finally cash in his ticket and buckle-up on a ride.

Now, the stakes of normal life are a lot higher than a single afternoon at Disney. YOLO (You Only Live Once) is a truism of pop culture. We all know that, as we age and mature, we are passing milestones, many of which cannot be revisited. Childhood, high school, raising a family, choosing a profession, retiring – many of these are experiences that slip through our hands like water. And behind them all, at the far rim of a life, is the shadow of death. This terminal experience is no serene merging into a placid ocean. It is something more like a violent plunge from a waterfall. Taking our last breath, we lose touch with the world as we know it and relinquish all of the treasures that we diligently collected and carefully preserved. In a flash, the ride is over, the ticket is used, and there is no second entry.[10]

In light of the unsettling fact of death, a key sign of spiritual maturity is appreciating the brevity and finitude of life.[11] Whereas a child who leaves an amusement park gets to go home and wake up to a new day, the game of life is not a repeated venture. Reincarnation is a myth. A man who wastes his life on meaningless pursuits is throwing something away that is unredeemable. This is why many philosophers have taught that consciousness of death is necessary to live an authentic life. Teenage boys are reckless precisely because they are oblivious. It is only because they are ignorant of the fragility of life and the finality of death that they are willing to bet everything on a leap off a bridge into murky water or a drag race through a congested street.

---

10. Ernest Becker captures the shock felt by death-awareness saying, "Man is literally split in two: he has an awareness of his own splendid uniqueness in that he sticks out of nature with a towering majesty, and yet he goes back into the ground a few feet in order to blindly and dumbly rot and disappear forever." See *The Denial of Death* (Souvenir Press, 2020).

11. An ancient poem ascribed to Moses says, "So teach us to number our days that we may get a heart of wisdom" (Ps. 90:12).

Grown men ought to have a more reflective attitude. No one throws expensive coins into a wishing well. The coins are too valuable to waste on a stupid superstition. Following the same logic, no adult man should toss away the priceless years of his life in a vacuum of insignificant pursuits. If we are only given a single ticket in life – one chance to pass through the present world – then adults should *adult* sufficiently to proceed with care. All of us want lives of meaning, purpose, and substance. Given this ineradicable desire, we have no excuse for allowing distraction or busyness to inhibit us from the task of measuring our choices against some touchstone of truth, goodness, authenticity, and honor. To disregard such responsibility is like a child wasting his ticket on a merry-go-round because he cannot be bothered to look and see if there are better options – *only magnified one thousandfold.*

So far, you have been advised to ask two questions. The first was, *Where am I going?* This was the question of a pedestrian. It is a simple question that anyone who drafts a life-plan should be able to answer. The next was, *Who am I following?* This was the question of a sociologist. It requires looking for the subtle yet potent ways in which society and culture mold our choices. Now, the third question is like the drop off from the shallow to the deep end of a swimming pool. Once the question is posed, you are no longer wading in mere observation. You are now treading in the deep waters of what the ancients called philosophy (literally, 'love of wisdom'). The question is this: *Is my life moving in the direction of real and lasting significance?* At the point you take up this thought, you lose any comfort that you might have felt before in simply fitting into the expectations of an inner circle. The point of reference for significance is no longer the expectations of other people, but something more transcendent and difficult to discern. You must now judge whether the altar of your 'god' is worthy of the sacrifice of your life.

There is no greater price than the cost of giving up one's life. Strangely, we often think that it is just the lot of heroes and martyrs to make what is rightly called the greatest sacrifice. Yet, the truth is that no human being can live without doing this. Each of us is inescapably a living offering to some transcendent and supreme value. It may be to success, country, pleasure, family, self, or "god." But the principle is universal: We all live for something, which means we all die for something. The man who lives his life for one night stands is just as much of a martyr as St. Stephen. The only difference between the two is the altar on which each one perishes.

In view of this spiritual fact, you need to be diligent to test the quality of your life. All of us live in Vanity Fair with only one ticket in hand. Countless voices around us are beckoning the gullible to empty their pockets for what amounts to nothing more than plastic trinkets and forgettable thrills. How can a man pass through so much marketing without making a fatally dumb decision? Step one is *thinking*. The Old Testament book of Proverbs says, "The beginning of wisdom is this: Get wisdom, and whatever you get, get insight." The recipe to escape foolishness, in other words, is detached reflection, sustained thought, patient listening, and self-analysis. No one can choose better until he has thought differently. We must step away from the noise of the herd so that we can figure out not just where we are going, who we are following, and what we are serving but – even more importantly – where we ought to be going, who we ought to be following, and which "god" is worthy of the sum total of my life.

Think Outside the Box

The fact that you are still reading indicates that you are agitated by the thought of robotically following a crowd. There is an interest growing in you to take responsibility for your life and to make sure that your conduct meets a genuine standard of significance and value. You see the herd as a threat, not a home. Thus, perhaps for the first time, you are thinking critically, even philosophically, about the trajectory of your life.

This marks legitimate growth. The difference between not-thinking and thinking is as great as the difference between sleeping and being awake. No one can self-direct without self-awareness.

Nevertheless, such progress is only an initial step in a long journey. Once you recover the dignity of detached reflection, you immediately encounter a problem. Let's label it "mental dimness." The mind is like an eye in that it depends on light to operate. If the mind has no input of truth (the spiritual equivalent to light), the mind is disabled. Your choices will be limited by what you *cannot* see as much as by what you *can* see.

This threat presents a massive stumbling block to today's men. A lot of us are like caterpillars living snugly in cocoons. We are content to be out of touch with the largeness of reality. Instead of exploring the full dimensions of existence, of truth, and of God, we restrict our minds to the dark and suffocating confines of what a materialistic society counts as the "real world." This inevitably stifles our freedom, imagination, perception, and capacity for growth. We can liken this to stepping into a grocery store and deciding to limit our shopping to a single aisle. Think of the difficulty of making a healthy dinner if the only ingredients in reach were shelves of snacks and candy. The moral condition of a lot of people in the twenty-first century is eerily similar to this. Our thoughts, ideas, and aspirations are limited to what is set within our intellectual reach by popular culture. No wonder so many of us feel emaciated! Our minds are operating on the equivalent of a popcorn diet.[1]

It's important to underscore that this cocoon-instinct is every bit as dangerous as the herd-instinct. If the herd-instinct keeps us from thinking for ourselves, the cocoon-instinct keeps us from living in the full light of reality. Detached reflection is of little value if the mind is blindfolded. Though the image is ridiculous, picture a caterpillar trying to find lasting fulfillment in the confines of a cocoon. It would lack the conditions needed to spread its developing wings and become what it ultimately is. We are in a similar predicament if we seek self-fulfillment apart from an earnest movement toward ever increasing dimensions of truth. Human

---

1. A lot of men will not realize that the original purpose of a liberal education was to *liberate* the mind. One was not free to pursue happiness until his mind was trained in the disciplines, virtues, and canons of truth. For recognizing just how non-nutritious the modern media environment is, no book is better than Neil Postman's abidingly relevant *Amusing Ourselves to Death* (Methuen Publishing, 1987)

existence is more like the emergence of a butterfly than many realize. If you are serious about finding authentic meaning and purpose you will need to undergo an experience not dissimilar to breaking through a restrictive shell. You will need to stretch out your mind like a set of wings and catch flight in the upper airs of topics and questions that many people defensively avoid – the upper airs, that is, of religion and philosophy.[2]

If this sounds confusing, the same problem can be addressed from a different angle. There is no shortage of men who parade themselves as religious and spiritual skeptics. They show no interest in the most ancient and profound of human questions. They will debate sports and politics with the passion of puppies wrestling on the grass, but ask them a question about the meaning of life, or a question about the nature of the soul, and they fidget like teenagers in a sex ed class. Somehow deep questions have become taboo questions in male chat. To drop "god" into a normal conversation has the same effect as flatulating in public. It is a social faux pas as awkward for the casual by-stander as for the culprit himself.

We need to ask the question, why is this? What is it about modern life that causes so many of us to be allergic to philosophic and religious thinking? How is it that questions which have fascinated the greatest minds for millenia are now received and discarded like cheap marketing on a busy

---

2. The great novelist Marilynne Robinson does a magnificent job exposing the narrowness of the modern conception of reality in *The Givenness of Things*. Among other beautiful statements, she says, "But anyone who has spent an hour with a book on the new physics knows that our old mechanistic thinking, useful as it is for so many purposes, bears about the same relation to deeper reality that frost on a windowpane bears to everything beyond it, including the night sky and everything beyond that." See *The Givenness of Things: Essays* (Virago Press, 2015).

street? Why is it that we can talk endlessly about scoreboards and injury-lists of a favorite team, but questions like, *what is happiness? what happens after we die?* or *what is the source and end of existence?* leave us with twitchy thumbs looking for something to scroll?

Now, I need to be clear that the task at hand is not to give a historical explanation of how men *de*volved into this bovine condition. There are any number of histories that dissect the progressive decay of Western society and offer insightful critiques of modern culture.[3] Our purpose is otherwise. The aim of this chapter is to disarm intellectual slothfulness. We want to rip open the snug cocoon of unreflectiveness so that the light of truth can touch your eyes – hopefully, awakening an appetite to go out and explore more of the brightness of reality surrounding you.

Why is this so important? Jesus gives the answer: "And you shall know the truth and the truth shall set you free" (John 8:32). His point is that freedom and truth are as closely connected as water and life. It will only be as you step out further into the rays of truth that you will discover what it means, *really*, to be alive.

The Cave 2.0

Long ago, Plato told a parable about the human condition. It begins with people chained in a cave. Behind them there is a fire with objects passing in front of the flames. These objects cast shadows on a wall, the shadows being the only things that people can see. No one in the cave has ever visited the

---

3. For men who want to explore this topic, three useful books are Jacque Barzun's *From Dawn to Decadence* (HarperCollins, 2000) ; Carl Trueman's *The Rise and Triumph of the Modern Self* (Crossway, 2020); and, for those that like fiction (and humor), Walker Percy's *Love in the Ruins* (Open Road Media, 2011).

outside world. Therefore, for all they know, the shadows on the wall are true pictures of what is real.

One day a man gets free of his chains and finds a way out of the cave. For the first time, he sees the world in its radiant goodness. Instead of shadows, he beholds objects in the clear light of day. Most impressively, he looks up and sees the sun itself, the magnificent source of light that illuminates the rest of the world. Amazed by his new experience of truth, the man goes back into the cave to tell others about what he has seen. Sadly, no one believes him. They refuse to accept that the shadows are insubstantial or that there is something as implausible as a light suspended in the sky.

The lesson of this parable is not difficult to glean: appearances are not reality, and the realm we identify as the "real world" is, in fact, a pale reflection of something more substantial and abiding.

Now, as insightful as Plato's allegory is, the truth is that the story has fallen behind the times. Therefore, for the sake of relevance, it needs to be updated.

Imagine that over the last 2,500 years a lot has changed in the cave. The cave is now lit up by electric lighting and has an efficient air conditioning system. Instead of staring at shadows on a stone wall, the people now watch digital images projected on flat screens. In addition, the cave inhabitants have discovered innovative ways of growing new foods and treating nasty diseases. The cave has gone from being damp, dark, and cold, to being dry, well-lit, and comfortable. Moreover, one further important change has happened: centuries ago, the people in the cave figured out that the shadows were mere *shadows*. They now laugh at the naivety of their ancestors. They pride themselves in being able to distinguish between a real object and a flight of fancy.[4]

---

4. Kierkegaard once wrote, "If it were not in one sense madness it

Every once in a while someone still disappears down a path and comes back with stories of having seen amazing things – of a higher world of indescribable light and beauty. But such reports are treated with the same scorn as before. In this TikTok version of the cave, no one cares whether or not higher dimensions of reality exist. The cave-dwellers are too comfortable and too amused to feel a need to explore beyond the stone walls around them. The passion to perfect the cave itself has quenched any desire to explore alternative frontiers elsewhere.[5]

Now, in light of these extra details, consider the following question: is the situation in the cave any different after modernization than before? In one sense, *yes*, in another, *no*. In terms of comfort, life in the cave has gone from crude and dingy to modern and snug. The new-fashioned cave is a palace compared to the hovel that existed before. Yet, in terms of wisdom, technological improvements have left the basic problem of the cave intact – *people underground still think and behave as if the cave is all that exists.* They are still reducing the complete field of reality to the set of objects that can be seen, touched, and measured in an underground cavern.

This may not sound like a big deal. I have no doubt that, hearing this, you may shrug your shoulders. You may think to yourself, "If such people are happy, why does it matter whether or not further truth is discovered? If the goal of life is contentment, and if men in the cave are content, why

---

would be a good example of humor if a man were to say to God: although I was strictly brought up as a Christian I was, as you know, born in the 19th century and so have my share of the universal superstitious belief in reason etc." The statement could be re-written for the twenty-first century substituting "technology" for "reason."

5. Tolkien tersely diagnoses modernity's brokenness as "improved means to deteriorated ends." See *On Fairy-Stories* (HarperCollins, 2014).

disturb the status quo? What's wrong with a daydream if the end result is peaceful and satisfying?"

Such spiritual indifference is not rare. In fact, it's the premise on which most modern lifestyles are built.

And yet, before you slump permanently into a "who-cares!" attitude, it's worth poking your incuriosity with a few questions. For example, what if the people in the cave were not, in fact, designed to live underground? What if their true fulfillment depended on feeling soft grass beneath their feet or being lost in wonder as they gazed at unreachable stars? What if the most delicious of pleasures required contact with something that could not physically be touched or seen? What if there were horses to be ridden and rivers to be fished – experiences that could not be manufactured underground? What if, in short, there was an infinitely better experience of life under the sun that could not be replicated by artificial lighting or virtual reality? If any of these hypotheticals were true, then the people in the cave would be just as stunted after their technological revolution as before it. Comfort could never be equated with freedom; amusement could never be substituted for fulfillment. For as long as a man lived in the cave, he would be like an infant in the womb: his environment would place a definite limit on his capacity for growth.

It is at this point that we can identify a hidden motive of indifference that a lot of men will be loath to consider. It is this: a lot of men use skepticism as a cloak to hide their intellectual and spiritual slothfulness.[6] One is hard pressed to

---

6. Dorothy Sayers is typically astute in dissecting slothfulness. She says, "[Slothfulness] means the slow sapping of all the faculties by indifference and by the sensation that life is pointless and meaningless and not worthwhile...it is the child of covetousness and the parent of...lust and greed." See her essay "The Other Six Deadly Sins" in *The Whimsical Christian* (Prentice Hall & IBD, 1987).

find a man who has diligently gone out to seek for truth, come back empty handed, and adopted the mindset of a skeptic after having carefully weighed the evidence. This is not how the typical agnostic is born. Instead, most men use the same tactics for discovering truth that they use for understanding politics. They don't read the editorials; they just scan the headlines. They don't have in-depth conversations with thoughtful friends; they listen to sound-bytes that affirm pre-existing assumptions. In other words, for a lot of men, skepticism is a product of the will, not a product of the intellect. Men choose skepticism as a spiritual defense because indifference means that they can enjoy the status quo without needing to worry about higher moral claims or deeper spiritual obligations. They can sit contentedly in the cave without a nagging thought that, by living underground, they are behaving more like moles than men.

Now, let me be perfectly clear about the main point here. The current objective is not to demonstrate (yet) a specific order of transcendent reality, but to disrupt the premature contentment of non-thinking men. Too many of us buy into the myth of secularism without ever questioning it. We act as if material comfort is the highest source of happiness and that, if you cannot see something, it does not exist. We ought to second-guess such assumptions. There are countless testimonies in history of noteworthy people who claim that the most lofty peaks of pleasure and fulfillment are above the foothills of what we can immediately touch or taste.[7] Such voices harmonize in telling us that a journey is required to reach such heights, one that involves diligent seeking, inward purification, and radical humility.

---

7. The only people who have said otherwise are the Epicureans who were a small minority for most of history until they strangely spread like a virus across the modern world.

In light of such possibilities, you need to engage in some self-interrogation. You need to take up the following questions: why not go on a search to see if there is a realm outside the cave? Is modern life really so satisfying that there is no itch to go out and look for purer springs of happiness and greener meadows of fulfilment?[8] Can ceaseless amusement truly cancel your interest in finding out whether there just might be something like a glorious sun towering over all, giving life and beauty, glory and grace, to everything under its rays? Life is frustratingly short. Many of our physical pleasures will perish as quickly as leaves in autumn. If rumors exist of a higher plane of meaning and hope, why not test the validity of the reports? What is so wonderful about a digital age that it could snuff out your passion to pursue what is the most ancient and noble of all quests, the search for truth?

If you reflect on these questions honestly you may be surprised by what you uncover. In a lot of cases, the roadblock to spiritual growth is not a skeptical mind. Real skeptics, after all, are known for asking questions.[9] The problem is

---

8. There is a sense in which the cave only functions because the majority of the inhabitants are complicit in a lie. The more one studies the advertisements of a materialistic culture the easier it is to believe that we are playing a universal game of pretend. Our collective behavior is a sign of pervasive misery, not plentiful joy. Through technology, we are numbing our pain and distracting ourselves – not because we are full – but because we are empty. Rather than being content and peaceful, we are depressed and fearful. The great secret of the cave – the thing everyone knows but no one is willing to admit – is that life in the modern world is as miserable as it is comfortable. The more advanced our civilization becomes the more we feel as if we are stuck on a ship that is sailing in the wrong direction. At our backs is fulfillment, happiness, and everything worthy of being called "home." Before us? No one knows. No one can see far enough to tell us where we are going.

9. The English word is derived from a Greek root that means investigation. In Classical Greek, a skeptic is an inquirer.

more likely to be a flaccid will. The spiritual appetites of a lot of men have been tamed by the soul-numbing thrills of a cold beverage and a cheap diet of dopamine. Like Esau, many of us have sold our birthright for nothing more than what turns out to be a bitter cup of broth.

Modern Pessimism vs. Ancient Optimism

If you are following the argument thus far you should be asking the following question: how can I be confident that the search for truth will not result in disappointment? This is no insignificant doubt. The stench of cynicism permeates the modern world. A lot of us have heard at one time or another the voice of a university professor reporting that the search for higher wisdom is a game of hide and seek that is impossible to win.[10] Such "experts" tell us that there are as many truths as there are cultures and that to look for any single truth – something worthy of a capital "T" – is not just foolish but dangerous. Truth-seekers, we are warned, are no different than the conquistadors who set out to find the fabled city of gold. They trample dissent in order to find something that is no more real than the gilded streets of El Dorado. The same voices argue that the only way to sustain human peace is to make truth relative, a matter of taste rather than verity. We are told that it is only after human beings give up on the quest for moral and spiritual truth that they will be able to coexist with differences and live together in harmony.

You need to handle such advice with extreme caution. Intellectual pessimism has a tendency to spread like a virus. Listen too long to the wrong channel on YouTube and the

---

10. Men should keep in mind Neil Postman's remark, "There is no idea so stupid that you can't find a professor who will believe it." See *Technopoly: The Surrender of Culture to Technology* (Vintage, 1993).

flicker of spiritual passion will be drenched by cynicism. At best, you will conclude that the hunt for truth should be something like a gentleman's hobby – a task to be performed at leisure, not a serious endeavor. At worst, you will lose faith in truth completely and one day feel the weight of your existence free falling into the chasm of a meaningless universe. More than one atheist has, in the end, lost his mind.[11] Sanity, as the Latin root of the word indicates, is not just being rational, but being healthy. The normal condition of the mind, as the near universal testimony of human cultures indicates, is not a mindset of radical doubt, but one of hopeful trust. Our deepest religious intuitions are not that the universe is silent and no one is speaking, but that someone is trying to get our attention and that the message is as personal as it is deep.[12]

It is at this juncture that you need to decide whether you will cast your lot with the pessimism of the modern world or with the optimism of a more ancient tradition. Up until not that long ago, people believed that finding wisdom was not just possible, but the great task, privilege, and responsibility of human beings.[13] Even if there were divergent schools of philosophy, and a range of cults and temples, underlying the differences was a shared conviction that some order of meaningful truth was accessible to us. The universe may

---

11. Nietschze is the obvious example.

12. Chesterton says, "Atheism is abnormality. It is not merely the denial of a dogma. It is the reversal of a subconscious assumption in the soul, the sense that there is a meaning and a direction in the world it sees." See *The Everlasting Man* (Moncrieff Press, 2023).

13. Aristotle gives the classic statement of this at the start of his *Metaphysics*. He says, "All men by nature desire to know." This intellectual appetite animated the classical world, the medievals, the renaissance, and the rise of modern science. Seemingly, it only died with the advent of mass, cheap amusement.

have been a riddle, but it was not a joke. There was meaning to be discovered if only the right set of keys could be found to unlock it.

It is within this tradition of optimism that we have the testimony of the book of Proverbs in the Old Testament. In this book there is a claim regarding wisdom that ought to excite modern ears. The statement is remarkable due to its brazen hope regarding the availability of truth. According to Proverbs, wisdom is not playing a coy game of Marco/Polo. The opposite is the case. Wisdom stands like a salesman with a megaphone trying to get our attention. In Proverbs, we read:

> Does not wisdom call?
>   Does not understanding raise her voice?
> On the heights beside the way,
>   at the crossroads she takes her stand;
> besides the gates in front of the town, at the entrance
>   of the portals she cries aloud:
> "To you, O men, I call,
>   and my cry is to the children of man.
> O simple ones, learn prudence;
>   O fools, learn sense.
> Hear for I will speak noble things,
>   and from my lips will come what is right,
> For my mouth will utter truth" (8:1-7).

Two ideas shine like headlights in this text. One is the picture of wisdom offering herself as a willing guide to anyone looking for help. This image ought to reinflate the hopes of those disheartened by intellectual despair. Truth, Proverbs is saying, is not a timid stag that flees the presence of the hunter as soon as it catches his scent. On the contrary, truth is waving her hands trying to be found. Like Arachne who helped Theseus escape the labyrinth of Crete, wisdom is in the business of helping disoriented men get out of the cave.

The second point of interest is that we ought to expect the search for truth to feel more like listening to a voice than looking at a map. It is worth pausing for a moment to think about this difference.

People often repeat the slogan "seeing is believing." For some strange reason, human beings seem to trust their eyes more than their other senses. Such naivety is surprising. Anyone who has studied modern journalism understands just how easily the eyes can be deceived. The problem with images is that, rather than containing 1,000 words, they do not, in fact, contain any at all. Often, having seen an image of a war scene or a hospital ward, we make flash judgments about the meaning of what we see. Such judgments are commonly incorrect. Seeing may be *believing*, but seeing is not *knowing*. In many cases, truth is deeper and more interesting than what the eyes can capture.[14]

This, in part, is what Proverbs is communicating by describing the guidance of wisdom as something heard, not seen. It's one thing to look at a map, see a comprehensive picture, and to move forward with the confidence of knowing precisely where you are and where you need to go. It's something different to hear a voice in a noisy crowd saying, "Follow me!" The first contains a high degree of certainty; the second, a high degree of trust.

Such trust is an essential first step in the path of truth. No reader of the Bible will be surprised by this. The start of the Bible operates on this vital principle. One of the marvels of Genesis, the first book of the Bible, is that the story of creation begins without any formal introduction to indicate much about who God is or why He should be trusted. Instead,

---

14. Jacques Ellul explores the degenerating consequences of prioritizing sight over hearing in *The Humiliation of the Word* (Grand Rapids: Eerdmans, 1985).

the opening pages of the Bible are like a bridge that one finds across a deep chasm in the middle of a trail. Instead of taking one massive leap of faith, a person is summoned to test his weight on the frame bit-by-bit, taking new steps only after previous ones have been proven safe and load-bearing.[15]

The passage in Proverbs is summoning us to travel on a similar step-by-step journey. Men in the 21st century are like bumbling tourists in a foreign city. Spiritually, we feel disoriented, lost, and confused. Yet, according to Proverbs, there is a presence who is trying to get our attention and who is saying, "I can help you." The name of this eager guide is Wisdom, and the path that she is trying to lead us along is Truth.[16] Her only initial demand of us is that we shift the posture of our hearts from one of pride, despair, and skepticism to one of humility, hope, and trust. In her voice we hear a promise: seek and you will find it; knock and the door will be opened to you. Her pledge is that there are answers to our deepest questions, and satisfactions for our deepest longings. Rather than existing in a silent universe, she coaxes us to believe that we are encompassed by a Word that is waiting – not just to be deciphered – but to be known, trusted, and loved.

---

15. This is not a claim about the doctrine of Scripture. This is merely an observation about what it is like to read the Bible for the first time. Even at the point one reaches the story about Abraham, so much is still unknown about God. He's there, but largely unknown. Like Abraham himself, the reader has to take repeated steps of faith as the story unfolds.

16. Wisdom is typically depicted as a woman throughout the ancient world. This rendering eventually becomes Lady Philosophy as evident in Boethius's classic, *The Consolation of Philosophy* (Penguin Classics, 1999).

Excursus:

AVOIDING THE PIT OF THE BIG ME

If you are willing to entrust yourself to Wisdom, there is one peculiar modern peril that you need to avoid. This is the pit of subjectivism.

The modern world is strange in that it tells us that the Holy Grail of meaning is lodged in the hidden depths of the self. Our fulfillment, so the lyrics of a thousand pop songs reverberate, is a prize won by discovering an inner voice, an oracle within that speaks infallibly on issues of authenticity, meaning, and fulfillment. The fundamental message of this modern attitude is "be true to yourself." According to this secular religion, happiness stands or falls according to whether we submit to our inner appetites or joylessly suppress them.[17]

There is good reason to question the safety of this path. As different as the cultures of ancient Greece and ancient Israel were, they agreed on one point. Both Abraham and Aristotle learned wisdom by turning outside of themselves, not inside of themselves. It's a tragic thought that a man could exhaust the whole of his life in pursuit of the Holy Grail, only to find out at the end of his quest, that the sacred treasure was located on a different continent. This is the warning that classic wisdom shouts to modern people. In Athens, wisdom began with wonder, the amazement that came from seeing the harmony and beauty of a starry sky. In Jerusalem, wisdom began with reverence, the trembling awe that came from hearing the authoritative voice of an invisible but Almighty God.[18] In spite

17. Taylor is unsurpassed in terms of diagnosing the secular identity. See *The Ethics of Authenticity* (Harvard University Press, 1992) and his magnum opus, *A Secular Age* (Belknap, 2007).

18. Leon Kass brings out this contrast in *The Beginning of Wisdom: Reading Genesis* (Free Press, 2003).

of all of their disagreements, Socrates and Moses would at least join voices to protest the idea that navel-gazing can lead to authenticity or any substantial sense of happiness.

We need to ponder the relevance of this older mindset. In Proverbs, as we referenced already, we read, "The beginning of wisdom is this: Get wisdom, and whatever you get, get insight." The word translated as "wisdom" in this quotation deserves attention. Wisdom is the appreciation of the meaning of something intelligible, whole, and complete. It is the ability to perceive structures and laws that give order to human life, not unlike the structures and laws that give order to the physical world. Wisdom says that humanity is not placed at random in a senseless universe, but placed meaningfully in what people once called a "cosmos."[19] According to wisdom, there is a grain to our design. We can either respect this pattern and find freedom and satisfaction or we can resist the design and experience deep moral and spiritual frustration. Thus, according to Proverbs, reducing wisdom to something subjective is every bit as ridiculous as trying to study and appreciate the sun by entering a closet and shutting one's eyes. The route to wisdom is not mysticism, but attunement. Just as a sailboat must be crafted according to physical laws in order to be able to stay afloat and navigate the seas, human beings will only flourish when we pay attention to spiritual dynamics that preexist us and are therefore inescapable.

19. For a Biblical understanding of this framework see Gerhard Von Rad, *Wisdom in Israel* (Trinity, 1970). For a philosophical and theological account of the same, see David B. Hart, *The Experience of God: Being, Consciousness, Bliss* (Yale University Press, 2013).

Achieve Moral Earnestness

We are still wrestling with a problem. It has been diagnosed already, but for you the treatment given thus far will only have been half of what is needed. In a word, the problem is *interest*. It's one thing to have the kind of interest that is exhibited when thumbing through movies on Netflix. It's something else to have the kind that Jesus depicts in the parable of a man who sells everything to purchase a single pearl. The first type is as superficial as an itch; the second is as deep as an obsession.

Now, more than likely, the first two chapters will only have tickled your curiosity. The discussion may have provoked a question or two about your life choices, but nothing revolutionary will have happened in your heart. No seismic shift will have demolished the foundation of your current lifestyle, leaving you looking in the rubble for a new rock on which to build your life. Instead, you will still be on the same path that you were on before. You will still be in the "cave" and probably still within the "herd." Absent from your conscience will be the pangs of urgency. There will be no sense of crisis, of standing before a decisive fork in the road, of a need to make a choice that just might determine the difference between a life fulfilled and a life squandered.

It is this laissez-faire attitude that needs further disruption. You need to feel what might be labeled the sting of truth.[1]

As a child, I remember once playing chase, and, while running full speed, tripping over a root. I flew head first into the trunk of a large oak tree. The impact was stunning. It took me a few moments to figure out where I was or what had happened. A similar effect ought to correspond to an authentic encounter with truth. Truth is every bit as firm and immovable as a thick and deeply rooted tree. If you are actively living in opposition to truth, then a collision with what is real and permanent ought to be a soul-rattling experience. If this does not happen, it is very likely for one reason: something has buffered the impact. The cushion may be distraction; it may be unclear and vague thinking; it may be an attitude of indifference; it may be the whirlpool of an uncontrolled life; it may be a combination of all of the above. Regardless of the cause, the problem is the same: personal contact with truth has been avoided.

The goal of this chapter is to make sure that such contact happens. For this to occur, we need a new tone and a new approach. The chapters thus far have functioned like a splash of cold water to the face. They were small jolts meant to arrest drowsiness. This chapter is more like a cold shower. It is designed to awaken you to a much higher level of alertness. Jesus once said, "Blessed are those who hunger and thirst after righteousness, for they shall be satisfied" (Matt. 5:6). The aim here is to push you from feeling peckish to being famished. For spiritual growth to happen, you need to achieve

---

1. You may remember that Socrates was called "the gadfly" because his questions were biting and pricked people out of comfortable ignorance.

a state of moral earnestness. It's not enough to be intrigued by truth; you need to feel as if you can't live without it. The present chapter is a midwife to help you reach this new state of being.[2]

How will we do this? The method will be to consider three truths that frame the moral existence of each and every one of us. These truths are like Newton's Laws of Motion: we can ignore them, but we cannot escape them. They are some of the most basic rules of the game of life which determine whether or not we have a chance to achieve what is the great prize behind all human endeavor: *happiness*. The three truths are the following: that there are only two roads in life; that every foolish choice is a forfeit of freedom; and that a man can only reject the invitation of wisdom so many times before her gentle voice goes terrifyingly silent.

Life Only Has Two Roads

Modern men are purebred consumers. We imagine that, in all areas of life, the ball is in our hands. We picture ourselves as intelligent, competent individuals. This is true of our spiritual existence as well as of our material existence. If we are going to consider a change of lifestyle, we picture Lady Wisdom in Shark Tank or Dragon's Den giving us – her judges – a sales-pitch. Her job is to persuade; our job is to decide. If she fails to convince, we retain the freedom to decline her offer and to shop elsewhere for a more intriguing product.

Now, it's not surprising that we have adopted this mindset given how intensively we have been educated in consumerism. The ecosystem of modern life is defined more by marketing than by any particular type of flora or

---

2. Using Kierkegaard, we could say this chapter is about pushing you from an aesthetic to an ethical stage of existence.

fauna.[3] At the center of this inextricable web of messaging are two big lies. The first is that the entire world revolves around the needs and desires of *me*, the independent self.[4] The other is that there are endless options in life and that we can pick a route to self-fulfillment like we can select a burger from the drive-thru menu at McDonalds. Sadly, men have downloaded these lies to the point of them becoming the operating software of their hearts. Thus, when it comes to pondering the big questions of life, we feel as if we are in a low-pressure situation. The voice of Wisdom is nothing more than one of many equal options to choose from. If we are bored or uninspired by what she says, we can ignore her counsel without any serious consequences or loss. Just as we can drive past McDonalds and take our business to Burger King instead, we can dismiss one bid for wisdom, trusting that another similar offer is just around the corner.

Most people from the ancient world would be puzzled by this default mindset of the modern self. The classical world was less polluted by crass consumerism than ours is. Thus, when people long ago thought about wisdom and truth, they didn't picture themselves as surrounded by options or sitting in a seat of quasi-divine authority. If there was a quasi-divine figure, it was Wisdom, not the self.[5] If there was a choice to be made, it was only between two options, not many – a choice, that is, between truth and error.

---

3. Terry Eagleton comments, "Civilisation is the world that is humanly manufactured. It involves rolling back nature to the point where we confront almost nothing in our surroundings that does not reflect ourselves. It is hard for us to recapture the novelty of this kind of environment." See *Culture* (Yale University Press, 2016).

4. George Elliot in *Middlemarch* writes, "We are all of us born in moral stupidity, taking the world as an udder to feed our supreme selves." (Wordsworth Editions, 1993).

5. In Proverbs 8 wisdom is given such an exalted status that, over time, theologians came to identify wisdom with a hypostasis of God.

Such a stark attitude is reflected in Proverbs, a book we have already visited. Throughout Proverbs, the complexity of human life is whittled down to two paths. One is labeled "wisdom," the other, "folly." Repeatedly, Proverbs dramatizes these paths as if they were living figures employed in competing marketing campaigns. On the one side, Lady Wisdom is crying out for men to follow the way of truth. We have already heard something of her message in the previous chapter. What we have not yet considered are the incentives that she holds forth to those willing to heed her guidance. In a justly famous quote, she says,

> Blessed is the one who finds wisdom,
>   And the one who gets understanding,
> For the gain from her is better than gain from silver
>   And her profit better than gold.
> She is more precious than jewels,
>   And nothing you desire can compare with her.
> Long life is in her right hand;
>   In her left hand are riches and honor.
> Her ways are ways of pleasantness,
>   And all her paths are peace.
> She is a tree of life to those who lay hold of her;
>   Those who hold her fast are called blessed (3:13-18).

Not much needs to be said about these incentives. They encapsulate all that the ancient world would have called "blessing" and what we moderns label "happiness." To live a wise life, Proverbs confidently asserts, is *to live* in the fullest sense of the term.

Yet, this is not the only sales call in Proverbs. Clashing with the voice of Lady Wisdom is the solicitation of Lady Folly. Her motives are as menacing as her tactics are bewitching. Proverbs says,

The woman Folly is loud;
    She is seductive and knows nothing.
She sits at the door of her house;
    She takes a seat on the highest places of the town,
Calling to those who pass by,
    Who are going straight on their way,
"Whoever is simple, let him turn in here!"
    And to him who lacks sense she says,
"Stolen water is sweet,
    And bread eaten in secret is pleasant."
But he does not know that the dead are there,
    That her guests are in the depths of Sheol (9:13-18).

Folly is pictured here as a heartless prostitute. She is persistent, enticing, and dangerous. She preys off the weaknesses of men, knowing that her glossy promises will result in deep and abiding dissatisfaction. No man with a fleck of gray hair is in need of outside testimony to confirm the pain that follows a one-night-stand with Folly. It takes very little experience in life to learn the grim lesson that, although stolen water is indeed sweet, such draughts are filled with a poison that quickly leads to bitterness, shame, and regret.

The simplicity of this ancient perspective – that life only consists of two options – is as relevant now as it was in the days of King Solomon. Although an ever-increasing number of voices are streaming through podcast feeds and digital advertisements, in and through all of them, only two voices are ultimately heard. Wherever there is truth, Lady Wisdom is beckoning; wherever there are lies, Lady Folly is flashing her red lights.

There are two implications of this moral predicament that you need to ponder. The first is that, whether you like it or not, a choice must be made. This choice is not between a wide selection of equally good options (or even a scale of variably rated items). Rather, you must picture yourself as facing a single road that can only be followed in one of two directions. You can either heed wisdom and turn your back to foolishness, or you can heed foolishness and turn your back to wisdom. No third option is available.

The second implication is that sitting on the fence and delaying a decision is a spiritual impossibility. This is, in part, due to the drift of modern life. You cannot shut your ears to the messaging around you. The noise is overwhelming. If you do not resolutely choose to heed the counsel of wisdom, wittingly or unwittingly, you will find your lifestyle being shaped by the advice of the culture around you. Sadly, in a broken world like ours, this means opting for folly. You need to know that wisdom is not the default position of the heart. The direction of wisdom is uphill. To move downhill is inevitably to amble in the direction of what Proverbs calls "Sheol," the realm of the dead.

Every Foolish Choice Is a Loss of Freedom

Western culture tends to separate the mind and the will. We think that we can choose to do something evil without this choice affecting our future ability to discern truth. For example, rare is the person today who fears that watching a little pornography or telling white lies will dim his moral understanding. We believe that moral vision is like physical vision; it is relatively stable and slow-changing. We do not worry that, if we ignore the voice of wisdom, this rejection of goodness might radically hinder our ability to perceive and embrace goodness later on.[6]

---

6. One of the most helpful philosophers and theologians on the moral relevance of habit is the great nineteenth-century Scotsman, Thomas Chalmers. See in particular his volume 1 of *Institutes of Theology* and *On the Power, Wisdom, and Goodness of God as Manifested in the*

If this idea is confusing, the principle can be illustrated with the image of playing a video game. Often, in video games, if a character fails in the attempt at completing some task, or reaching some level, the game will restart at the point of failure. The obstacles do not change; neither do the abilities of the character. The point of the game is to keep playing until failure turns to success and a given mission is accomplished.

Now, we often approach our moral lives with what might be labeled a "video-game mindset." We imagine that we can commit a moral failure (i.e., give into a temptation or act on an evil desire) without such failure having a detrimental impact on us.[7] This is why a lot of men have an indifferent attitude when it comes to the "small" moral tests in life. We feel as if we can consent to the appeals of Lady Folly without such indulgence costing us much, if anything. In the same way that a video game character like Mario can "die" and restart the game where progress stalled, we can "sin" and restart life afterwards without any notable loss of freedom, strength, wisdom, or self-control.[8]

You need to appreciate just how naive this mindset is. If we are going to use a video game analogy to make sense of our moral existence, we need to imagine a game in which, each time the character on the screen fails, the game becomes a bit harder to play. The conditions of such

---

Adaptation of External Nature to the Moral and Intellectual Constitution of Man. Both available digitally. Much of this section is a reflection of this thinking.

7. The opposite is also true. We don't tend to think that resisting temptation, or choosing virtue in the face of vice, might strengthen our character and enlighten our minds.

8. Samuel Johnson gives a vivid allegory of the loss of freedom through vice in *The Vision of Theodore, the Hermit of Teneriffe, Found in His Cell.* Available online.

a game would not be stable, but ever-changing according to the performance of the player. Rather than getting lots of opportunities to restart a level at the same point of failure, after each defeat the character would be set back slightly and his powers atrophied. In such a game, lots of careless mistakes could quickly result in a near impossible field of play. Consequently, each new test would need to be approached with circumspect care and deliberate thought. Indifference would be a recipe for despair. Only those players who were emotionally invested in the game would have any chance of success.

Such a presentation of life as a dynamic and ever-changing field of play is precisely what we find in the book of Proverbs. In Proverbs we read,

> The path of the righteous is like the light of dawn, which shines brighter and brighter until full day. The way of the wicked is like deep darkness; they do not know over what they stumble. (Prov. 4:18-19)

The picture of moral life depicted in this statement is one of a path that either progressively brightens or darkens. The difference between the two outcomes is the moral and spiritual quality of an individual's choices. On the one hand, if we take steps of "righteousness," our perception of what is good and true will be illuminated just a bit.[9] On the other hand, if we choose "wickedness," the light will dim. Such light, if ignored, can eventually be snuffed out altogether, leaving a man in a frightful state of enveloping darkness.[10]

---

9. Chalmers says, "Evil deeds and the indulgence of evil affections serve to thicken that film which has settled upon the mental eye, and obscures its every perception of the truths of revelation." See volume 1 of his *Lectures on Romans*.

10. Jesus captures the danger of moral darkness in the Sermon on the Mount when he says, "But if your eye is bad, your whole body will

What Proverbs here is urging you to pay attention to is the inextricable link between the will and the mind. To see the good and yet choose evil does not leave the mind intact in a stable condition of moral health. Deliberate "sin" (a concept to be explored in more detail later) is a real cause of moral blindness. Once you understand this connection, you ought to feel the urgency of heeding the voice of Lady Wisdom. Unlike video game characters, you don't get multiple tries at overcoming a moral challenge from the exact same position. Each failure is a setback in the most literal sense of the word. If you reject the guidance of wisdom, you cannot be assured of having the same aptitude to hear her voice the next time she calls. Each step toward darkness is, in truth, a step away from light. Each act of moral rebellion – tacit or deliberate – is a net loss of moral freedom.

This dynamic reiterates the inescapable truth that no man can be spiritually stagnant. Each one of us is either spiraling upward in the direction of light or spiraling downward in the direction of darkness. Pausing at the twilight of good and evil is not an option for anyone.[11]

If You Reject Wisdom, Wisdom Will Reject You

Imagine going to a car lot and talking to a salesperson. You hear a lot of interesting information about a new model of car that sounds like it might be a good fit for your family. The specs are good, and the price well within reach. Yet, for some reason you decline the offer and go home.

A month later you decide that you want to revisit the lot. You drive to the location only to discover that the cars are

be full of darkness. If then the light in you is darkness, how great is the darkness!" (Matt. 6:23).

11. Jesus issues the following warning: "For to the one who has, more will be given, and he will have an abundance, but from the one who has not, even what he has will be taken away" (Matt. 25:29).

no longer there. Like a circus, the entire business has been packed up and moved elsewhere. The deal that you were hoping to make is gone and irretrievable.

It's important to know that you cannot have wisdom on your own terms. Moral insight is not something on tap that can be turned on and off at leisure. Wisdom is more like rain that falls at uncontrollable times. You either collect and use wisdom when it's available or else you miss the fleeting opportunity.

Such is the meaning of the parable above. You must realize that, if you reject wisdom, there is a real possibility that wisdom might ultimately reject you. There may come a day when you go looking for an insight that was previously available only to discover that the voice that was once heralding loudly on the street corner has now packed up and moved elsewhere. This may sound similar to what has already been said regarding the dynamic way in which each man is progressing either toward light or toward darkness. However, a shift of perspective needs to be noted. We are talking now, not about the inward state of a man, but about the external availability of truth. Truth has the uncanny ability to hide itself such that a man who previously had access to light suddenly finds himself lost in overwhelming darkness.

This terrifying possibility is something that Proverbs is quite clear about. In Proverbs, we see a striking shift in the tone and message of Lady Wisdom after her invitations have been repeatedly rejected. In the face of ongoing scorn, she says,

> Because I have called and you refused to listen,
>   have stretched out my hand and no one has heeded,
> because you have ignored all my counsel
>   and would have none of my reproof,
> I also will laugh at your calamity;

I will mock when terror strikes you,
when terror strikes you like a storm
    and your calamity comes like a whirlwind,
    when distress and anguish come upon you.
Then they will call upon me, but I will not answer;
    they will seek me diligently but will not find me.

(1:24-28)

The final lines ought to horrify you if you are toying with an attitude of spiritual indifference. A lot of us are okay with a degree of danger. We will happily smoke a cigarette or speed down a highway because the risk of such actions is perceived to be small. This same attitude can easily carry over into our moral lives. We think that rejecting a spiritual intuition is like drinking too much on a single Saturday night. We may feel hungover the next day, but one night out is not a recipe for liver cancer. In a similar way, we're not worried that a single moral slip might result in a condition of helplessness.

It is such nonchalance that Proverbs is trying to shake you out of. The warning of ancient wisdom is this: To pass up any invitation to exit the cave may unintentionally be a choice to stay in the cave forever. The voice that is presently urging you to move toward a higher realm of freedom, truth, and joy will not endure your aloofness indefinitely. Like a spurned suitor, she will eventually give up and move on. Such are the high stakes of the moral responsibility of human beings. A careless vote for folly could result in folly governing the heart *permanently*.

Ice-Bath for the Indifferent

So what if you are still shrugging your shoulders after all of this? What if you don't feel that much motivation to get up from the cave and to go out searching for the truth? So far we've splashed some cold water on your face (chapters 1 and 2) and offered something more like a cold shower (the three main ideas in this chapter). Is there something akin to an ice-bath – a more painful remedy to snap you out of the lethargy of indifference?

If this is the case, I can offer one last tonic. I do so hesitantly, because there are dangers attached to what I am about to advise. This counsel is a last resort; it is only for you if you feel as if each and every spiritual nerve in you is numb. Here is the advice: *stare nihilism in the face.* If the beauty of the light is not enough to awaken earnestness, then perhaps the horror of beholding nothingness might just be enough to spark a longing for something more.

Here we can learn a lesson from Nietzsche. Nietzsche, more loudly than anyone else, calls the human bluff of skepticism. He notes how quickly we kick God out of the front door only to sneak in a new "god" through the backdoor. Most atheists are hypocrites in this respect. They claim to reject God when, in fact, all they do is rename Him.[12]

If you are going to be indifferent regarding truth, you need at least to have the courage to consider the implications of existing without truth. The fact is that a lot of men buffer their consciences by living in the afterglow of a religious world. In other words, they hang on to some of the comforts of religion without believing in any of the doctrines that originally gave consolation and meaning to the human soul. As a child clings to a blanket, these men hang on to a belief in the dignity of personhood, the hope of something after death, the security of a higher hand at work in the world, and the sacredness of moral values like justice, mercy, and love. Yet, such beliefs smell of cowardice. A man who has no interest in the pursuit of truth should not allow himself the comfort

---

12. For more on the surreptitious ways in which this is done, see Terry Eagleton, *Culture and the Death of God* (Yale University Press, 2015).

of living in an order of truth. We cannot have our cake and eat it, too. Either there is moral and spiritual truth in the universe that provides consolation and meaning to human existence, or there is not. If such truth does indeed exist, then awareness of such reality ought to govern the interests of our lives. Happiness will depend on discovering and conforming to a spiritual order of being. Conversely, if there is no such truth, then you need to accept the implications of what it means to be a brittle reed in a dark and silent universe. You need to accept that morality, justice, meaning, dignity, and hope are nothing more than beautiful myths. Without truth, there is only one creed that stands the test of logic: "Eat, drink, and be merry, for tomorrow we die."

Are you still indifferent about spiritual things? Here is some candid advice: stare honestly into the darkness of nihilism. Turn off all artificial lighting and noise and feel the vacuum of nothingness. Let the specter of death draw close enough to you so that you can see its black eyes and feel its cold breath. If the recoil of horror, angst, and despair is not enough to stir you to look for something more, I'm not sure what can. The man who consoles himself in the arms of death is a man who has lost his will to live.

Excursus

THE POWER OF SEEING-ONESELF-AS

Identity is one of the most powerful motives for human action.[13] The more we identify ourselves with a cause, a group, or a character, the more frictionless our choices flow in the direction of an ideal. The man who views himself as a competitive athlete will naturally find it easier to wake up to exercise or to abstain from ice cream than the person whose identity is altogether detached from fitness. There are few reservoirs of human motivation more potent and renewable than *seeing-oneself-as*.

This rule has important implications for you as you undertake the itinerary of this book. On the one hand, if you identify with the right type of character, you will find a stable interest to stick doggedly to the path of wisdom. On the other, if you identify with the wrong type of character, your feet will struggle to move in any direction other than foolishness.

Now, one of the helpful lessons of Proverbs is that, when it comes to facing the crossroads of wisdom and folly, there are only three types of men. These can be labeled scoffers, sluggards, and sons.

In Proverbs, a "scoffer" is the name of an arrogant and haughty man who believes that he can live independently of wisdom (cf. 21:24). Scoffers "hate" wisdom (cf. 1:22) in the sense that they have no need of it. The trinkets that they are after – power, sex, status, comfort, and money – can be acquired more efficiently by other means. Therefore, wisdom is held to be a dispensable commodity.

---

13. James Clear is very good on this point, See *Atomic Habits: Tiny Changes, Remarkable Results* (Penguin, 2018).

Proverbs is clear that there is no point in trying to admonish a scoffer. Proverbs says, "Whoever corrects a scoffer gets himself abuse" (9:7). To try to teach a scoffer is like trying to convince a workaholic to rest. No problem is felt; therefore, no remedy is needed. Sadly, this means that the only moral hope for a scoffer is brokenness – the acute pain experienced when superficial sources of happiness and significance unexpectedly and irrecoverably collapse. Yet, even this is sometimes not enough to shatter the hubris of a scoffer. Proverbs warns, "He who is often reproved, yet stiffens his neck, will suddenly be broken beyond healing" (29:1; cf. 19:29). The point here is not just that pride comes before a fall. Something more weighty is at stake. Pride is a deadening of moral faculties. To entertain pride for too long is like allowing a disease to linger which can ruin health permanently.

The second type of person is the "sluggard." The sluggard is someone who hears the invitation of wisdom and says, "Perhaps tomorrow." The sluggard can always think of a reason to delay a decision, no matter how ridiculous the excuse may be.[14] The root weakness of the sluggard is a complete lack of initiative. Proverbs says, "As a door turns on its hinges, so does a sluggard on his bed. The sluggard buries his hand in the dish; it wears him out to bring it back to his mouth" (26:14-15). The image is meant to be comical and repulsive at the same time. Sluggards really are *losers*. Any man whose highest ideal is to live by a cheap recipe of amusement and comfort is *losing out* on the possibility of experiencing anything worthy of being called *joy*. This is why Proverbs speaks of the sluggard as being in a "deep sleep" (19:15). Just as a person who is dreaming is out of

---

14. Proverbs 26:13 says, "The sluggard says, 'There is a lion in the road! There is a lion in the streets!'"

touch with reality, the bodily appetites of the sluggard cause him to disassociate from the higher aspirations that could give weight, nobility, and meaning to his soul.

In the end, the fate of the sluggard is no better than that of a scoffer. Proverbs says, "The desire of the sluggard kills him, for his hand refuses to labor" (21:25). The relevance of this quote is much broader than a mere regurgitation of Aesop's fable about the ant and the grasshopper. Men must labor, not just for food, but also for wisdom. If we are not willing to grapple with questions, and if we are not willing to search diligently for answers, we will end up spiritually destitute and emaciated. Slothfulness, as a long tradition of moral philosophy warns us, is indeed a deadly sin.

The third possible identity is that of a "son." Now, to understand this we need to delete everything we have learned from modern culture about what it means to be a son and what it means to have a father. For men in the contemporary West, our emblems of sonship and fatherhood are the anemic figures of Bart and Homer Simpson. Our assumptions are that dads are nothing but children in big bodies and that children live most fully when they rebel against their dads. Such beliefs are toxic. They dismantle the goodness of a true father-son relationship, one that needs to be recovered if we are going to understand the ideal posture of the soul before wisdom.

Fortunately, Proverbs offers us a different perspective on the virtues of sonship. In Proverbs, being a good "son" is about listening carefully to sound advice and yielding oneself to well-tempered wisdom. Being a son is having the humility to admit personal ignorance, incompetence, and immaturity and having a supple heart before trustworthy voices of wisdom, discernment, and sound reasoning. The heart of sonship is seen in the following quotation:

Hear, O sons, a father's instruction,
  and be attentive, that you may gain insight.
for I give you good precepts:
  do not forsake my teaching.
When I was a son with my father,
  tender, the only one in the sight of my mother,
he taught me and said to me,
"Let your heart hold fast my words;
  keep my commandments, and live.
Get wisdom; get insight …
Prize her highly, and she will exalt you;
  she will honor you if you embrace her (4:1-5a, 8).

The point here is not to focus on the precise content of wisdom, but the attitude that men ought to display before her. The best picture of this is the posture of a meek son before a respected and much-loved dad. If we approach wisdom with such reverence, we have every reason to be encouraged. Her willingness to honor us will be no less than a father's willingness to honor his son.

Now, you need to take these three profiles and use them for self-analysis. You need to ask yourself – not which label best describes your past behavior – but which one best describes your aspirations? Do you see yourself as a scoffer, sluggard, or son? This is no mean question. How you answer it may well determine the outcome of reading this book.

Face the Truth about Yourself

This is not a book; it's a journey. Recall how far you've come. Not long ago your spiritual vitality amounted to little more than sitting in a dark cave, staring at a screen. One word could describe the state of that part of you that old thinkers used to call the 'soul', *asleep*. You were unthinkingly following a herd, trundling along without asking any questions about where you were going or why you were going there.

But, in recent days, something has begun to happen. A spiritual tinnitus has been ringing in your ears. Cutting through the noise of life, you have heard the still, small voice of wisdom saying, "This is the way; walk in it." At first, the sound was an irritation, like the buzz of a nagging fly. Yet, the irritation has heightened to a state of agitation. You now feel an urge to get up and strike out in a new direction, to find a path through the darkness that just might lead you to a higher life.

This book is designed to be a thread for you to follow out of the cave. There is an old fairy tale about a young princess who is given a special ring by her fairy godmother with a silver thread attached to it. She is told, whenever she is afraid, to put the ring under her pillow and to follow the thread wherever it might lead. The thread, she is told, will always take her back to safety. This is a useful picture to keep in mind as you keep reading this book. Most books are about downloading information. Not this one. The aim here is to trace a path of wisdom, which is more of an itinerary than a mere set of ideas. The path we are outlining is a set of experiences, which, if undergone, result in nothing less than spiritual growth, perhaps even new birth.[1]

Now, let's say that you do indeed begin to follow this path. What should you expect during your upward ascent from the cave? Initially, you will feel the enthusiasm of a new adventure, the excitement of taking steps of moral progress. You may feel as if the voice of wisdom gets just a little bit louder each time you take a further step in the direction of truth. There may be a sense of the proverb being fulfilled: "The path of the righteous is like the light of dawn, which shines brighter and brighter until full day" (4:18).

But it is here that I need to issue a warning. In the fairy tale mentioned above, there is a moment where the princess hears a loud noise and is afraid. She follows the advice of her godmother and begins to trace the thread into the darkness. At first she is exhilarated by the experience of being led out into the open night and up along a mountain trail. But eventually the thread leads to the mouth of a cavern, along a maze of underground tunnels, and, finally, smack into a stone barrier. Lost and trapped, she is terrified. She has gone from the comfort of her bedroom to what looks and feels like a dungeon.[2]

---

1. Jesus says, "Truly, truly, I say to you, unless one is born again he cannot see the kingdom of God" (John 3:3).

2. The entire story is worth reading, especially for refurbishing a

This story is related because, if you follow the voice of wisdom, there will be a moment when you feel the unexpected impact of something like a stone wall. This barrier will put a stop to any progress you are making in the direction of freedom and truth. It is not unlikely that you will feel a wave of dread hit you as you face up to a situation that is justly labeled impossible. This is a barrier that Plato did not foresee in his telling of the myth of the cave. In fact, no one from the ancient world grasped the extent of this stumbling block besides the Hebrew prophets and their later successors, the apostles of the early church.

What is this impasse? In a word, it is the problem of "sin," that condition of brokenness, corruption, and disorder that modern intellectuals have worked so diligently to whitewash, justify, explain away, and ultimately deny.[3] Some men, no doubt, will be put off by the mere mention of the word "sin." They need to second-guess their preferences – at least if they are honest about their desire for wisdom and personal growth. Anyone with one eye open can see that evil is not an imaginary problem. The biggest obstacle between "me" and happiness is not ignorance, but the human propensity to self-destruct. Mr. Hyde is always lurking within Dr. Jekyll. There is something inside me, you, us, and the entire world that defies rational explanation or self-restraint.[4] This havoc-wreaking propensity is too important to ignore. We can no

---

moral imagination. See George Macdonald, *The Princess and the Goblin*. Available online.

3. Malcolm Muggeridge famously said, "The depravity of man is at once the most empirically verifiable reality but at the same time the most intellectually resisted fact."

4. In *Moby Dick,* Herman Melville writes, "We are all cracked on the head and desperately needing mending" (Wordsworth Editions, 1992). This understands the traditional understanding of the human person as inherited from a Jewish, Christian past.

more disregard "sin" and expect spiritual growth than an addict can ignore compulsive behavior and expect peace and contentment.

Now, this chapter is all about self-awareness, not in the sense of self-monitoring, but in the sense of truthfulness. Most guys refuse to look honestly at their own reflections in the mirror. They play up their virtues and downplay their vices. They immerse themselves in too much noise and busyness to take stock of the collateral damage of their life choices. Any number of women and children may lie whimpering around them due to "boyfriend," "husband," and "father" wounds. Yet, none of this catches their attention. Ask them if they are good guys or bad guys, and a snap judgment provides the answer. They feel *good enough* – not because they have weighed up the genuine merits of their deeds or character – but because they are not as bad as the guy next door.

The aim of this chapter is to help you to strip down in order to take more objective measurements. Undergoing this scrutiny will not be fun, but it is necessary. "Sin" really is an impasse on the way to moral growth. There will be no way out of the cave until you face up to the massiveness of the brokenness within you. Ironically, it will only be after you feel completely boxed in and trapped by the presence of "sin" in your life that you will once again hear the voice of wisdom leading you toward freedom. One of the strangest truths in life is that hopelessness is very often the womb of hope. It is only after admitting we can do nothing to fix ourselves that an uncanny power begins to move toward us with a strength that exceeds the scant resources of the self.

Recovering the Testimony of Conscience

Everyone knows the problem of evil. Any cynical teenager can formulate some version of the question, "How can a transcendent source of wisdom, power, and goodness exist if there is so much pain and suffering?" For many, the most cogent proof of the nonexistence of "god" is a picture of a starving child in Africa. There is something about the cultural software of the Western mind that finds it nearly impossible to believe that suffering can be a part of a wise and good, albeit mysterious, design.

Yet, if we are honest, our thinking on the topic of good and evil is exceedingly narrow minded. There is a famous experiment in which psychologists show people a white piece of paper with a black dot on it and then ask the question, "What do you see?" In almost every instance, people reply, "A black dot." The experiment demonstrates the bizarre human tendency to fixate on select details while ignoring a much larger context.

This tendency is evident when most people contemplate the so-called "problem of evil." Are there dimensions of evil that ought to trouble the human conscience? Undoubtedly. Still, if we are willing to survey the full landscape of our experience, we must admit that evil is, at most, a splotch against a bigger backdrop. In fact, one can easily demonstrate that there would be no "problem of evil" unless there was first a "problem of goodness." Our deepest intuitions indicate that we are born, not just in a world of material substance, but in a world where goodness preexists us and determines the quality of our actions. Just as a black dot is only visible because it is set against a white piece of paper, in the same way, evil is only noticeable and deplorable because we judge it against a standard of what is right, just, and good. A monkey can contentedly live in a world of privation or violence and feel no moral pang that something is upside-down. Humans, on the other hand, are scandalized by the morally fractured world that we've inherited because some deep sensitivity tells us that things ought to be different. If we condemn acts of violence, greed, and hatred, it is only because we are in agreement that kindness, generosity, and love ought to be the principles governing our interaction.[5]

This human sensitivity to acknowledge the goodness of the good and the evilness of evil is what traditionally has been labeled the conscience. This unique human faculty bears testimony to a truth that is often suppressed and ignored in the modern world – namely, that moral laws are every bit as real and basic to human existence as are physical laws. We can no more argue that murder is good, or that theft is just, than we can argue that rocks are soft, or that light is darkness. There are indelible lines separating good and evil, and while we may debate on where exactly to trace the line, no man seeks to erase these boundaries altogether. To attempt, even for a moment, to live without such lines is to have a whistle blown and a red card allotted. The conscience scolds us as often as we need reminding that there is a real path of righteousness and that to deviate from this path is to incur the stain of guilt and the filth of shame.[6]

Yet, the conscience is more than a mere radar that identifies the lines of good and evil outside of us. The testimony of conscience is more introspective and personal than this. Through the conscience we become aware of an unnerving truth. The more closely we look at the black spot in the middle of the piece of paper, the more clearly we come to see that the spot is, in fact, a set of fingerprints that each must recognize as *his own*. Here it is helpful to think of conscience not just

---

5. C.S. Lewis provides a concise and cogent rendering of this argument in *The Abolition of Man* (widely available in collections of his work). This book is essential reading for men who need to be convinced of the givenness of truth and goodness.

6. In Romans 2:15-16 Paul speaks of an internalization of the law of God on the hearts of men. Conscience, he says, bears witness to this law.

as holding one office but many. When it comes to the moral quality of our lives, conscience plays the role of impartial witness, meticulous prosecutor, inflexible judge, and clear-sighted jury – all in one. With brutal honesty, the conscience tells us that no man can look to heaven and blame "god" for the problem of evil. The real guilt lies closer to home. Rather than being innocent bystanders of a crime scene that we had nothing to do with, our hands are dirty. Even if the riot of evil began before we arrived on location, we, too, are at fault. Here the surveillance tapes of our memories do not lie. Rather than stop the spread of evil, we have contributed to its destructive presence in the world. To use very unfashionable labels, instead of being "righteous," *I am a "sinner."* This is the unsettling truth that the faculty of conscience preaches loud and clear.

Refurbishing the Concept of "Sin"

There is an irony in modern culture. No society has ever been more interested in discovering new concepts to make sense of human experience and to improve life. The TED stage is a self-proclaimed platform of "ideas worth sharing." Likewise, the recipe of a successful podcast is to fill episodes with new ideas that will tweak mindsets and dispel mystery. Given this appetite for useful concepts, you would think that "sin" would garner more public interest. Rather than being a dusty word too embarrassing to bring out in public, "sin" is actually a necessary concept for making sense of normal life. Imagine trying to speak clearly about the idea of health without using words like sickness, injury, or death. The task would be impossible. Something similar is true for our spiritual lives. There is no way to speak of human wholeness or happiness without acknowledging the reality of "sin." If life is a journey through a beautiful but dangerous landscape, "sin" is a word that helps us to understand the various hazards that threaten to keep us from reaching happiness, which is the governing aspiration of every human heart.[7]

Now, the best way to understand "sin" is to drop the English word and to replace it with more ancient concepts that are rooted in a different moral framework. In English, the word "sin" carries a lot of unhelpful baggage. In contemporary speech, the word communicates a sense of polite naughtiness, of extreme pleasure, or of petulant moralism, none of which is useful for understanding the problem of human evil. Therefore, in order to get past our modern biases, an alternative path is needed for recovering the profound relevance of "sin."[8] Such a path is available through looking at the Old Testament. In the Hebrew Bible, there are three main words used to talk about "sin." Each one highlights a different aspect of the moral dimensions of human action. In each, we see how the darkness of evil is a problem only because it is framed against a larger, pre-existing canvas of light.

The first word is "*hattat*." Literally, the Hebrew word means "missing the mark." This image of being off target is extremely useful for reframing how we think about our spiritual lives. In bygone days, people were educated in what were called "virtues." Such virtues were marks of excellence. A man could either live up to the ideals of courage, justice, self-restraint, and wisdom, or he could fall short of them. The one thing he could not do was to redefine the target.

---

7. David Brooks works hard to dismantle the naive optimism of contemporary culture and to reintroduce older moral concepts in *The Road to Character* (New York: Penguin, 2016). See also Francis Spufford's *Unapologetic: Why, Despite Everything, Christianity Still Makes Surprising Emotional Sense* (London: Faber, 2013).

8. An alternative path to understanding the relevance of sin would be to consider the seven deadly sins.

There was a prevailing sense that the standards of excellence were like the rules of a game: they pre-existed the players and determined the meaning of fair-play.[9]

"Hattat" reminds us that this older picture of morality is a signpost to the truth. There are indeed various marks of behavior that human beings are designed to meet. These standards of excellence precede us and are above us. Something like generosity is not a mere cultural value. It is an unassailable good. One can either be generous or be greedy. What he cannot do is to argue convincingly that Ebenezer Scrooge is a better model of humanity than Francis of Assisi. The life of Scrooge, at least up until his Christmas intervention, was fundamentally off target. He had missed the mark, not just in terms of a set of actions, but in terms of life as a whole. Francis, on the other hand, was much more attuned to the spiritual dynamics of human life. He understood the inescapable principle that it is better to give than to receive.

The second word is *"pesha."* The word has the sense of a moral trespass, a spiritual overstepping of boundaries. It's interesting to contrast this idea with modern concepts of freedom. In today's world, we often think of freedom as unrestricted choice. Rules are considered to be stifling and oppressive. The sexual revolution is a classic example of this mode of thinking. The idea behind the movement was that, by removing boundaries to sexual behavior, people would be free to achieve greater fulfillment and happiness. Sadly, those carrying this so-called banner of "liberty" never considered a simple truth – namely, that good rules can actually preserve happiness rather than impede it. No one driving a car longs for the day that all traffic codes will be abolished. The result

---

9. This conception of sin dovetails with the description of virtue in Alasdair MacIntyre's *After Virtue* (London: Duckworth, 1981).

of "total freedom" would be chaos, not liberty. The same principle operates in morality. A lawless world is not a realm of unbridled freedom, but one of unbridled appetite. And anyone who has experienced addictive behavior can attest that appetite can be every bit as oppressive and controlling as a legalistic regime.[10]

More positively, "*pesha*" indicates to us that the world is, in fact, drawn up with moral boundaries. Rather than being "free" to do what we please, and go where we want, there are lines that are meant to restrict our movement. These lines are not oppressive, but protective and liberating.[11] They indicate something far more important than where *not to go*. They map for us the boundaries within which we are most free. A clear line between good and evil is not a fence that keeps us from discovering greener pastures. The opposite is the case. A good boundary is like a warning sign that signals where green pastures turn into dangerous bogs and precipitous cliffs. To commit a "*pesha*" (a moral trespass) is like ignoring a sign that says "Danger Ahead!" Such lawless acts are not expressions of freedom, but of recklessness.

A third word is "*avon*." This word reveals the way in which human evil is a moral pollution that contaminates both the world outside of us and the inner self. Although evil may not have a physical substance like a chemical, it does leave a kind of residue that is difficult to mop up and remove. The emotional experiences of guilt and shame are inner testimony to this truth. When we commit evil, we often feel

---

10. Edmund Burke says, "It is ordained in the eternal constitution of things, that men of intemperate minds cannot be free. Their passions forge their fetters." The quote is found in one of his letters.

11. The Psalms often capture this point by describing God's law as providing a broad and level path, free of obstructions, to be followed. Psalm 119:45 says, "And I will walk in wide space for I have sought your precepts."

as if there is a stain on our persons. The "sin" attaches to us leaving us feeling dirty and in need of an inward cleansing. We feel as if we need to do something to scrape off the filth of our deeds.[12]

The social dynamics of *"avon"* are also interesting. The sense of being unclean often drives us to hide from other people due to feeling unworthy of revealing ourselves – that is, the truth of our souls – to them. It's not accidental that the story of Adam and Eve eating the forbidden fruit results in them manufacturing cheap garments for themselves and hiding. This is the effect of human evil. Due to shameful actions, we come to view ourselves as a kind of spiritual untouchable who cannot show face among others. The pain of this experience can be excruciating. There is no shortage of people using substances or relentless activity to numb themselves because consciousness of moral impurity is too painful to bear.[13]

Now, this discussion of "sin" should feel like tin foil on a rotten tooth. Many a theologian has made the comment that "sin" is one of a few religious truths that can be verified by experience. We don't need to read a sacred text to become aware of two basic points: first, that there is a definite line between good and evil and, second, that (for some mysterious reason) we often choose to camp out on the wrong side of

---

12. The Old Testament book of Leviticus is an incomparable guide to much of what is being said about sin. Two helpful guides that cull out the moral framework of the book are Jacob Milgrom and Jonathan Sacks.

13. Gabor Mate has brought out the link between pain and addiction more forcefully than anyone. Alain de Botton picks up the same idea, writing, "What properly indicates addiction is not *what* someone is doing, but their way of doing it, and in particular their desire to avoid any encounter with certain sides of themselves. We are addicts whenever we develop a manic reliance on something, anything, to keep our darker and more unsettling feelings at bay." See *The School of Life: An Emotional Education* (Penguin, 2020).

the line. The latter point needs to be emphasized. It's easy to think that the difference between living "inside the cave" and "outside of the cave" is merely the difference between being ignorant and being enlightened. But this is not the case. A predilection for darkness is not just a problem of the mind, but a problem of the will. In life, each of us consistently chooses actions which are off-target, out-of-bounds, and self-corrupting. Such behavior is unique to humans in the animal kingdom. Whereas every other creature happily lives according to its nature and keeps within its design, we routinely defy our nature and disregard the moral habitat within which we thrive.[14] No eagle would give up its stately perch in the sun in order to hang upside down in a cavern like a bat. Yet, spiritually, this is exactly what we do. We exchange the better for the worse and live in darkness when we could be soaring in the upper breezes among the clouds.

Why is this? "Sin" is the concept we need to pinpoint the condition. Beneath the "*hattat,*" the "*pesha,*" and the "*avon,*" there is something more deeply wrong with us. The algorithm of our hearts is glitched. We are not just "sinners" in the sense of people who occasionally commit "sins"; we are "sinful" in the sense of there being something corrupt at the core of our being. Although we long for true freedom and happiness, our choices do not fall in line with our aspirations.

One of the first people to accurately diagnose this condition was the Jewish rabbi and Christian teacher, Paul of

---

14. For a deep dive on the depravity of human beings, no work is better than John Owen's classic, *Indwelling Sin in Believers* (Modern Puritans, 2023). He helpfully shows how the order of a lot of human action is the opposite of what it should be. Rather than the mind discovering a good, the will choosing it, and the emotions delighting in the choice; often the reverse process happens. The emotions hold the will captive and the mind is reduced to a contractual role of justifying a miserable state of affairs.

Tarsus. Two thousand years ago, he wrote, "I have the desire to do what is good, but I cannot carry it out. For I do not do the good I want to do, but the evil I do not want to do—this I keep on doing ... What a wretched man I am! Who will rescue me from this body that is subject to death?" (Rom. 7:18-19, NIV). Such frustration is common to man. We are the strange creature that insists on choosing what we know is self-defeating. This propensity is evidence of a kind of inner death. Our will is moribund. We lack the power needed to live by what is good, noble, and righteous. For this reason, we cannot cast the blame for evil on anything external to us. Although the problem of evil may be bigger than any single individual, no individual is disentangled from the problem. We are not merely spectators of the evil which is destroying our world; we ourselves are agents of destruction.[15]

Sin: Not Just a Problem, but a Danger

Now, there will be a reaction in you to the concept of sin that needs to be preemptively addressed.[16] You may read this far and think to yourself, "Who cares! I like the thrill of stepping out-of-bounds sometimes. I'd rather feel the residue of a little moral dirt than be spiritually OCD."

This attitude is not uncommon. It's a cliche of pop culture to describe hell as being a more interesting place than heaven. The message has sunk into the psyche of a lot of men. Deep down, a lot of guys worry that too much goodness is a bad thing. There is a feeling that life needs a little sin like food needs a little salt. To live a life devoted to moral purity would

---

15. Chesterton's famous answer to the question, "What's wrong with the world?" was the simple retort, "Dear Sirs, *I am.*"

16. At this point, I will no longer use inverted commas for "sin." The meaning of the term should now be sufficiently clear.

be like eating egg whites all of the time. Such an existence would induce a spiritual form of nausea.

Such sentiments need to be inspected. I'll never forget hearing a speaker say to a group of men, "The problem with men is that they don't think enough about sex." At first, I thought the speaker was disturbingly out of touch with his audience. But his point was more profound than I realized. His message was that, although men obsess about the act of sex, they rarely spend any effort thinking about the meaning, design, or purpose of sex. Consequently, the moral perspective of a fifty-year-old man is often not much more sophisticated than that of a recent high school graduate.

This problem of *not thinking enough* is a general weakness among men. This point needs to be reiterated because no man will sober up about the reality of sin unless he is first willing *to think*. Moral growth is not a product of following one's gut. The man who submits blindly to his instincts is doomed to a perpetual childhood. The only way to avoid such stunted growth is to dig up one's spiritual assumptions and to analyze them in the light of truth.

Now, if you believe that sin and "happiness" are in any way causally linked, you need to ponder two basic facts of spiritual life. One is the intrinsic connection between sin and pain; the other is the addictive power of yielding to any evil passion.

Sin Is Pain

This statement may sound counterintuitive. After all, a lot of traditional sins are intensely pleasurable activities. If they were not such, people would not do them. In fact, as has already been pointed out, the Bible itself admits, "Stolen water is sweet, and bread eaten in secret is pleasant" (Prov. 9:17). This means that the burden of proof rests on the claim – not that sin is enjoyable – but that sin is painful. A little extra spadework is needed to demonstrate the truth that whatever sweetness sin may have is, at most, a sugar-coating for something bitter and poisonous at its core.[17]

To see this, the place to begin is recognising the relationship between human actions and passions. Every action is motivated by one or more passions. These passions can be compared to the powder charge used to fire a rifle. Without some propellant, a rifle cannot fire. In the same way, there are few, if any, actions that are *unmotivated*. This connection is obvious in relation to sins. For every evil action, there is a preceding evil passion. For example, violence is usually the result of anger; slander, the byproduct of envy or spite; adultery, the consequence of lust; binge-eating, of gluttony; and so on. In each case, the sin would not occur if there was no passion. Just as a bullet only fires because there is a substance to ignite, sin only happens because there are passions latent in the soul.

Now, there is no denying that a lot of the actions produced by evil passions are enjoyable, at least in the short-term. Bullies get a thrill out of bullying just as womanizers get a thrill out of womanizing. Yet, such short-term pleasures do not prove that sin produces any substantial, genuine, or lasting happiness.[18] The real misery of sin is seen, not at the level of actions, but at the level of passions. An evil passion

---

17. Thomas Chalmers is excellent in showing the inherent connection between both pleasure and virtue and pain and vice. See his treatise *On the Wisdom, Power, and Goodness of God* (HardPress, 2018) Also available online.

18. There are numerous philosophers that dismantle the notion that immediate pleasure is a means of true happiness. Two useful guides are Boethius' *On the Consolation of Philosophy* and Thomas Aquinas. Aquinas's discussion can be found in 1.2.2 of his *Summa Theologica* (Catholic Way Publishing, 2014)

is no more capable of producing sustained joy than a disease is. In fact, each of the evil passions is nothing more than a way of labeling a unique kind of sickness that pertains, not to the body, but to the soul. All of them are simply different names for one thing: misery.[19] Happiness is not – and cannot be – composed of evil passions; it consists, rather, in their opposites. The man of peace and contentment is not ruled by anger, greed, or gluttony; he is under the reign of love, generosity, and self-control.[20]

As evidence, consider the following thought experiment. Traditionally, there are seven deadly passions that are the source of sinful behavior. They are anger, lust, greed, gluttony, sloth, envy, and pride. Now, picture a random person and imagine that any one of these passions has become the driving motive of his actions. In other words, this person does not just occasionally have an outburst of anger; he is an angry person. He does not just succumb to a rare mood of envy. He is enveloped in a cloud of unhappiness every time he steps among peers. He is not just sexually excitable; he is a sex addict. He does not just enjoy a good meal; frankly, he can't stop eating.

---

19. Dante vividly portrays this truth in the punishment of gluttons in Hell where they are consuming muck while being pelted with frozen rain. Dante's point is that the problem with sin is not that people desire too much, but too little. Their desires are their punishment. To be subject to a sin like gluttony is to be trapped eating mud pies in a cold downpour. It's not a happy experience. The same could be said of any of the other deadly sins.

20. Chalmers comments, "But God hath so formed our mental constitution, and hath so adapted the whole economy of external things to the stable and everlasting principles of virtue, that, in effect and historical fulfillment, the greatest virtue and the greatest happiness are at one." See *Wisdom, Power, and Goodness*. Anyone who is uncertain of this principle should work through Chalmers's extensive and intricate reasoning.

Once such a person is clear and distinct in your mind, reflect on the following question: to the degree that any one of the deadly passions takes hold of the existence of a man, will he be more happy or less happy? Will he experience more freedom or less freedom? The answer should be obvious. Sinful passions do not promote human happiness. The thought experiment pinpoints a basic moral principle that universally applies to human experience. Although sinful acts may result in short-term pleasure, sinful passions result in long-term misery. Who, after all, would actively seek after more anger, spite, greed, or gluttony in his life? We may like the thought of accumulating wealth, but we loathe the thought of becoming greedy. Sex is intoxicating, but men rarely want to become what used to be called lecherous. We may enjoy the feeling of being in the limelight, but no man actively pursues the goal of becoming a narcissist. The fact is, although we like the instant gratification that comes with some moral trespasses, we don't like the thought of such sins becoming rooted in our character. There is no more frightful thought than the possibility that a man's soul could be reduced to the following seven traits: anger, lust, greed, gluttony, sloth, spite, and pride. Such is not the portrait of a man; such is the portrait of the devil.[21]

If you are still unconvinced of the point, there is one final (though perilous) way to demonstrate it: devote one month to acting on the deadly passions of the heart and record daily the results of the experience. Each day you will feel a bit hollower and a bit more rotten inside. Greed, gluttony, and lust are no more able to produce peace, joy, and contentment than rocks can produce flowers. It's simply not in their nature.

---

21. Joseph Conrad shows the dehumanizing effect of evil in *The Heart of Darkness* (Legend Press, 2020). It's a scary thing to look at the life of anyone controlled by evil passion.

The short-term pleasure of sin will ineluctably give way to long term pain. You will feel yourself deteriorating from a man to a ghost. Life will slowly feel as if it is dissolving. You will taste for yourself the undeniable truth of a principle that the Apostle Paul outlined two-thousand years ago: "The wages of sin is death."

Sinful Passions Are Addictive

A careful reader will identify a flaw in the preceding argument. You will consider that sin is more like alcohol than poison. Alcohol cannot be consumed in a pure state; however, in a diluted form, alcohol is enjoyable. Sin, you may suggest, is similar. There is a qualitative difference between being a sex-addict and stoking the embers of lust. The one is a set of chains; the other, the spice of life.

This counterargument, though clever, is invalid due to a hidden assumption, one that has already been addressed in various ways. This is the misconception that it is possible to exist in a morally static condition. We should recall here the faulty picture of our moral existence as a kind of video game in which we get to start over repeatedly at a point of failure. When we adopt this mindset, we imagine that, for example, we can consume some light porn without this indulgence altering the shape of our character. There is no fear of a hardening of habit; there is no worry about a loss of freedom. We consent to the passion convinced that we will be in the same state after the moral trespass that we were in before.

Such a mindset ignores one of the most fundamental rules of human character, namely, the law of habit. A helpful way to think about this law is to imagine a person holding his two wrists out in front of him, one beside the other. Each time a moral compromise is made, picture a very slender rubber band being placed around both wrists. Now one, two, even three rubber bands, will be easy to break and will not restrict a man's freedom to move his hands. Yet, consider what would happen if, repeatedly, new bands were placed over the wrists. At some point, a threshold will be crossed after which a person will no longer be able to separate his hands. There will be a point at which they will be functionally glued together.

This illustration demonstrates the problem with thinking that sin is not dangerous in a diluted form. When we think of human character, we should never think of something that is static and unchanging. All of us are snowballing in one of two directions. Either we are being transformed according to what is good, and thus experiencing more freedom, or we are being changed into the likeness of what is evil, and thus forging a personalized set of shackles. Maintaining a moderate balance between good and evil is no more possible than trying to be a healthy bulimic. One is either being transformed into the likeness of goodness or into the likeness of evil.

Thus, instead of thinking of sin as a bottle of single malt, to be sipped sparingly, a better image of sin is something like a spiritual narcotic. There is no doubt that a hit of cocaine or a jab of heroin might provide an exhilarating high. Yet, when most people think of these substances, they think not only of potential pleasures, but of perilous risks. We ought to have the same mentality with sinful passions. Only a fool would think of sin in terms of the question, "Is it fun?" The wise man confronts temptation – not by asking a question – but by looking at a price tag. He sees clearly that sinful indulgence is always purchased at the cost of freedom, peace, and joy. He understands that no one gets to draft the terms and conditions for consuming sin. Like a casino, sin is happy to hand out an early payout. But this is not without a strategy. The game is rigged so that the initial payout will induce a further temptation – and as one temptation folds into another – the house always wins.

Step into the Light of Holiness

We have hit upon a problem regarding moral growth. This is the problem of the evil that resides within the human heart. The path to self-transformation is not just outlined by growth in knowledge (the intellectual ability to distinguish between light and darkness), but also by growth in goodness (the willingness to choose light instead of darkness). And herein lies the problem. A strange sickness afflicts human beings such that we often prefer to loiter in the shadows than to stand in the warmth and light of the sun. The depth of this depravity is profound. Plato thought that human beings choose wrongly due to ignorance. If we could just see the truth more accurately, we would live more justly. But Plato was naive. Our sickness has corrupted our appetites and desires. Somehow, we have developed a taste for what is lethal. Even after reading the warning labels on forbidden fruits, and even after experiencing the convulsions of imbibing poison, knowledge lacks the strength needed to curb desire. We live wrongly, not just because we think wrongly, but because we love wrongly. We are not birds that have accidentally flown into a cave and somehow gotten trapped. Such creatures would readily exit the pitch dark given an open window. We are bats that have evolved to feel at home in a cave. We don't leave the darkness because, sadly, we like it.

This is the obstacle that impedes our ascent to a higher life. It's somewhat strange that in the modern world this point needs to be made at all. Up until recently, a basic pillar of the Western worldview was the "fallenness" of human nature (often labeled "original sin"). In talking about this, theologians and philosophers did not mean that human beings were incapable of doing good. The arts and sciences are evidence enough that there is a nobility that is inextricable from our nature. The point, rather, was that human beings are like broken musical instruments. The best music we produce comes forth distorted and perversely short of the beauty and goodness of which our design is capable.[1]

Now, if you are unsettled by the depressing turn that this journey has taken, you need to be forewarned. The diagnosis of our condition is about to get even worse. I say this in order to appeal to an inner sense of fortitude. There are two types of men that will have made it thus far in this book. One is driven by mere curiosity, a superficial hope to find cheap principles for self-improvement. If this is you, it's time for you to close these pages and turn elsewhere. Dante famously imagined the gates of Hell being inscribed with the words, "Abandon hope all ye who enter here." A slightly modified warning should be attached as a prelude to this chapter: "Abandon all *superficial* hope ye who enter here." Readers must understand that wisdom does not pay dividends to the half-hearted. It is not the tourist, but the pilgrim, who finds truth to be his guide.

---

1. The classic treatment of original sin is Jonathan Edwards' work *The Doctrine of Original Sin* (Available online).

The other type of reader is a man who is driven by a nagging spiritual pain. He presses on, not because of any expectation that the journey will be easy, but because to turn back is to give up on life itself. Like the central character in *The Pilgrim's Progress*, he looks at the world around him and sees a City of Destruction. What feeds his desire to plod on is a disgust for the vanity of the culture around him and a deep intuition that something transcendent, even eternal, is latent in the world, waiting to be discovered. Such a man does not need hard truths to be softened or bitter self-criticism to be sweetened. He is willing to face reality so long as there is hope that the outcome will be cleansing and redemptive.

This mindset is what I mean by fortitude. There is a distinct kind of courage needed to inch ever closer toward the penetrating light of truth. According to the gospel of John, the condemnation of most people is that "the light has come into the world, and people loved the darkness rather than the light because their works were evil. For everyone who does wicked things hates the light and does not come to the light, lest his works should be exposed" (3:19-20). Such exposure is the fear that drives most people away from incisive self-analysis. To stand in the light of truth is not to see the reflection of a majestic and beautiful "me." It is to come to terms with the fact that what ought to look like an image of a god instead looks like the emaciated figure of a ghost.

A lot of men will shrink back from this realization. The loss is theirs. The light of truth is indeed painful to look into, but it is also purging. It is only by drawing near to the fire of truth that our uncleanness is burnt away and our pride melted down into a substance that can be recast into the shape of something sacred and noble.

Now, the purpose of this chapter is to shift the focus from sin to holiness. This change of perspective is needed in order to do justice to the barrier inhibiting our progress toward a higher life. The truth is that the problem of sin is not just subjective (something in the soul), but relational (something involving the ground of all personal reality). Until we understand what it means to exist in the presence of the Holy One, we will never adequately grasp the predicament of sin. We will make the mistake of thinking that sin is merely an inner brokenness to be fixed by therapy or spiritual discipline. The critical insight we will lack is that sin is not just a condition; it's a verdict. It's not just a broken heart; it's a stance of rebellion.

We need to understand this in order to build a framework for understanding what is required to escape the fallen plight of man. The "cave" is more than a state of ignorance or even depravity. To be in the "cave" is to be hiding from the presence of a justice that is threateningly severe and uncompromisingly righteous. In other words, to be in the "cave" is to be hiding from God.

In the course of this chapter we will rethink what it means to live in the light of divine glory. You need to be patient in doing this. Nothing in the secular world prepares us to think rightly about God.[2] Thus, the challenge before us is to recover the mental scraps left over by modern culture and piece them together in some way that does minimal justice to a foreign dimension of reality. How will we do this? Our method will involve three steps. First, we will imagine a

---

2. C.S. Lewis famously said that his imagination was baptised by reading the fiction of George MacDonald. Modern men can baptise their own imaginations by reading the fiction of C.S. Lewis. For an unforgettable taste of holiness, men should read *Perelandra*, the second volume of Lewis's splendid Space Trilogy.

higher realm of life and light; second, we will imagine the experience of stepping out into the light of holiness; and, third, we will consider the experience of facing a justice as firm and inflexible as a mountain of granite. Only at the end of this process will you understand what it truly means to be in the "cave."

The Realm Beyond the Cave

To awaken to spiritual truth we must reimagine reality. We can do this by dividing existence into two realms.[3] One is the "upper realm" of truth and freedom; the other is the state of life that we have labeled the cave. The cave is an image of normal life in the modern world. It is a condition of mistaking shadows for reality and darkness for light. Yet, it is more than this. It is also an existence of living for immediate gratification, unfiltered appetite, and unrelenting distraction. A man can walk down random streets across the world and see countless people who are unwittingly inhabiting the cave. Such is the given condition of man. To be born into the world is to be born into a kind of moral and spiritual coma, even death.[4]

In contrast, the "upper realm" is a label for an alternative mode of existence. It represents a condition of having the freedom to live by genuine goodness, of experiencing deep moral satisfaction and fulfillment, and of achieving

---

3. All learning requires the process of initially using available concepts and then subsequently dismantling them in order to move toward a more accurate understanding. I'm not suggesting that "two realms" is an accurate way to describe reality. I'm simply using the concept to give the mind initial traction. Eventually, we will need to move on to more adequate ideas.

4. There are many films that try to capture the inauthenticity of our given existence. Two well-known examples are *The Matrix* and *The Truman Show*.

an authenticity that holds up to the test of truth and of righteousness. One of the fascinating things about the Bible is the way in which it speaks about eternal life. When most people hear the term, they immediately think about an afterlife – some disembodied condition of peace or joy on the other side of death. The Bible certainly does have plenty to say about a horizon of life that extends indefinitely beyond the reach of death. Yet, when Jesus, in particular, is speaking about eternal life, he often refers to something that has both future and present aspects. He depicts eternal life as a kind of new birth that can break into a mortal existence and cause fresh life to emerge as dramatically and irreversibly as a baby coming out of the womb.[5]

This idea of a present experience of eternal life is useful for conceptualizing the difference between what we are calling the upper realm and the cave. It is important to understand that, in the present world, there are two parallel modes of existence – one might even say two spheres of life intersecting. One is characterized by light, the other by darkness; one by life, the other by death; one by joy, the other by sorrow; one by hope; the other by despair; one by peace, the other by fear; one by love, the other by isolation; one by fullness, the other by emptiness; one by holiness, the other by sin. It is the reality of these competing realms which shifts all that we have been saying about the cave from being an intriguing fiction to being an existential fact. The reality is, the condition of every human being is defined by one of these poles of existence. We are either moving from a lower

---

5. To give one example, Jesus says to the Samaritan woman, "Everyone who drinks of this water will be thirsty again, but whoever drinks of the water that I will give him will never be thirsty again. The water that I will give him will become in him a spring of water welling up to eternal life" (John 4:13-14).

life to a higher one, or we have sunk to a condition that is, in truth, a form of bondage. Such is the drama of everyday life. Beneath the surface of routine tasks is a spiritual migration whereby every soul is transitioning toward a final state of being. We are all pilgrims. The question is whether we are moving in the direction of life or of death.[6]

It is at the verge of this insight that the problem of evil can be understood more profoundly. Most of us imagine that, if there is a higher realm of existence, then we have every right and incentive to go to this realm and participate in the blessing on offer there. We assume that, if we are in the cave, and there is a place where the sun is shining, all we need to do is to follow the right steps and we will soon be outside of the darkness and basking in the delicious warmth of a summer's day. If there is a need to attain a higher degree of purity, or to reach further stages of enlightenment, such barriers are surmountable with a little grit and education. Modern people are incredibly optimistic about their spiritual potential. We really do believe that our spiritual problems are resolvable so long as we have sufficient willpower and the latest gleanings on life-management theory at hand to enable us.

The naivety of this mindset is a stumbling block to growth. In truth, we are no more competent for handling our spiritual problems than a cancer patient is competent for removing a lethal tumor. We don't just need good advice to get out of the plight we are in; we need the radical intervention of a

---

6. In *The Moviegoers*, the great Catholic novelist Walker Percy writes, "The search is what anyone would undertake if he were not sunk in the everydayness of his own life. To become aware of the possibility of the search is to be onto something. Not to be onto something is to be in despair."

higher power that people in a more religious climate used to refer to as "grace."

To validate this point, two journeys of the imagination need to be undertaken. These will come in the form of "What if?" questions. The imagination is a potent tool for tilting a worldview. We often picture the game of life in a particular way because no one has ever shown us that the pieces on the board can be arranged in a better pattern. This is where the imagination is uniquely adept. There are few lines of thought more provocative than asking, "What if?" The question forces us to leave the safe walls of our uncontested assumptions and to step out into the uncertain space of what-might-be. By staring out into the realm of possibility, we make ourselves vulnerable to fresh insights – even revelations – of what is in fact the case. In this way, the influence of the imagination is like the magic wardrobe of Narnia. It enables us to step out into lost dimensions of reality, an experience which, if undergone, can leave us changed forever.[7]

What If Holiness Is Real?

You may be familiar with the character Gollum in *The Hobbit* and *The Lord of the Rings*. One of the striking features about this character is the toll taken on him by a prolonged existence of living in both a physical and moral cave. The effect of such deprivation is a grotesque distortion of his appearance, appetites, and dispositions. Having lived in the shadows for countless years, he becomes a shadow of his true self. He is a living gargoyle who is as appalling morally as he is physically ugly.

---

7. Paul Ricoeur is the great philosopher of the imagination. For Ricoeur, the imagination is not an alternative to perception but an ingredient of perception. See Ricoeur, "Lectures," 2:6 in *Sense and Sensibilia* (NewYork: Oxford University Press, 1964).

Now, just imagine that a creature like Gollum, on a whim, decides to venture outside of his den in order to enjoy the pleasures that are available in the outside world. He decides that he would like to pick some flowers in a meadow, to mingle among other creatures, and to see his own reflection in a puddle of water. This in mind, he journeys out from his underground home until he reaches the fresh air of the upper realm. Now, ask the question: Given the physical and moral mutations in his being, will he be able to enjoy the good things in the world at large? Will good things still be experienced *as good* by him, or will his changed character mean that he is no longer able to appreciate the qualities of a better life?

The most plausible scenario is the following: Upon exiting the cave, Gollum will quickly be made aware that he is no longer fit for the public world. This will be true for several reasons.

First, having lived for so long in the darkness, his eyes will be weakened and no longer able to withstand the brightness of a normal day. The sun will not be a source of refreshment; its light will be piercing and oppressive. Second, his appetites will have degraded. Good things are only pleasing if a creature has the tastes needed to appreciate them. Long years of nibbling raw flesh will mean that Gollum's tastes will have degenerated. Having gnawed on rancid bones, the sight, smell, and taste of a cooked dinner will no longer have any appeal. Third, his stature and appearance will have decayed. If Gollum did, in fact, get the chance to take a look at himself in a mirror, the result would be shame and horror. The contrast between the memory of who he was and the ghostly reflection of who he now is would be traumatizing. And, finally, due to the deterioration of his behavior as well as his figure, there will be no chance of Gollum being able to socialize among other creatures. His evil passions will have all but deadened the nerves of compassion, benevolence, and friendliness. He will no more be able to enjoy others than others will be able to enjoy him.

So, then, what would happen if a creature like Gollum suddenly stumbled out of a cave into the open air on a summer's day? Like a spooked deer, he would flee back into the shadows looking for relief from a foreign and threatening world. His brief exposure to the upper realm would entrench the belief that the cave was indeed his home and that he could no more exist under the transparent gaze of the sun than a fish could live in the sand.

This parable helps us to think soberly about the moral and spiritual journey that we are undertaking. There is a word in the Bible that has no parallel in modern culture. This is the word "holiness." The concept has many facets. One is the idea of a realm that is set apart from all that is common and unclean. Holiness is the space where life, purity, goodness, and joy exist in their fullest forms. In other words, holiness is the special dwelling place of *God*. The only things that are able to participate in the realm of the holy, other than God, are things free from any hint of evil, corruption, and decay. To stand in the realm of the holy in a state of moral uncleanness is a bit like standing naked in the court of a great king. It is an experience of excruciating shame – not to mention danger.[8]

It's important to know that, according to the Bible, human beings were designed originally with the dignity and innocence needed to live in the presence of holiness. In fact, we can say more. Such a spiritual habitat is our home; it's

---

8. Matthew Thiessen does a very helpful job reconstructing the framework of holiness in *Jesus and the Forces of Death: The Gospels' Portrayal of Ritual Impurity in First-Century Judaism* (Baker, 2021).

where we flourish and find our deepest satisfaction. Yet, the problem of human sin is a lot like the problem of Gollum's degraded nature. Both due to our own choices, and the choices of those who preceded us, we are no longer free to enjoy the life on offer in the realm of the holy. For creatures in a fallen condition as we are, holiness is threatening, not enlivening. To step out into the space of absolute holiness is like being dropped into the atmosphere of Mars. The condition is beyond what we are able to cope with.[9]

It's worth tracing in further detail why this is the case due to the degree to which modern people are unschooled in spiritual truths. Naively, we tend to think that notions of holiness are ideas that human beings impose upon the world around them like traffic lines on a road. Yet, this is not the case. Holiness is not an arbitrary social construct, but a permanent and inescapable dimension of reality. When we turn our minds to holiness, we are talking about something, like electromagnetic fields, which shapes our experience regardless of whether we affirm its existence or not.[10]

A further way to picture holiness is as a realm of special light. This light is nothing less than the presence of divine glory. Just as natural light unveils a world that is already present and there to be known, holiness is the unveiling of God. The overwhelming experience of being in the realm of holiness is awareness of God himself. He is like a brilliant sun shining overhead. All of the rays of what is good, true, and beautiful issue from Him. To stand in His presence is to

---

9. A book that makes this point convincingly is *The Concept of Holiness* by O.R. Jones. (G.Allen and Unwin, 1961)

10. The great Rabbi Soloveitchik writes, "Creation is an act of tolerance on the part of God; He bestowed grace upon something by allowing it to share his reality. God received the world into His 'lap' ... creation is bound and enclosed within." See *Worship of the Heart: Essays on Jewish Prayer* (Ktav, 2003).

behold the sheen and feel the heat of dazzlingly magnificent moral purity.[11]

Now, if the human heart were completely righteous, it would have the cleanness needed to gaze into the blaze of divine glory and to experience the ecstasy of beholding the infinite source of goodness and love. But this is where we fall short. One effect of sin is a decaying of our moral vision. Rather than being eagles, once thought to be able to stare directly into the brightness of the sun, we are now more like moles who dig underground to avoid the glare of daylight. It is worth noting that such aversion to divine light explains why God so often "feels" distant to people. The reason His presence goes undetected is not because His glory is not shimmering all around us. The problem is not on His side, but on ours. Each time we choose what is evil, we shut our eyes a little tighter and dig a little deeper underground. No creature can burrow into sin and see in the light of holiness at the same time. With each moral action, we either open our eyes or close them to the reality that is beneath, above, and before all things, namely, God.

Yet, there is more that can be said about the light of holiness. Light is exposing, and the brighter the light, the more darkness stands out in contrast. In a pale twilight, a speck of dirt can go unnoticed. In a flash of white light, the faintest spots of grease and grime stick out as garish stains. You need to appreciate that holiness is the highest pitch of moral light. To stand in its presence is to go through a spiritual MRI. The hidden tissues of evil are detected and brought into focus. This is why the thought of a sinful human

---

11. This truth is dramatically communicated in the way in which seraphim in the Bible shield their faces from looking directly into divine glory. Not even sinless angels can behold the naked glory of the living God.

being strolling out into the light of God's presence ought to terrify us. To stand before God with an impure heart is something far worse than being stripped naked in the presence of a king. A better image is that of a leper, someone whose flesh is repulsive to see, being stripped naked and having to stand in the presence of angelic glory. The shame would be unbearable, which is why the image of Gollum fleeing back into the cave is no exaggeration for the recoil of an imperfect man facing the inaccessible light of God.[12]

Still, more can be said. The effect of sin goes far beyond diminishing our moral vision. In addition to this, we need to recognise the way in which our appetites have been defiled by sin. Although holiness is the realm of the highest goods, such things are only pleasurable to creatures who have the purity of heart needed to enjoy them. The sad truth is that habituated vices make us incapable of being satisfied by holy pleasures. This is one of the highest costs of sin. Take, for example, the man who has submitted to lust as a ruling passion in his heart. The very essence of lust is to reduce the dignity of persons to consumable objects to be used and disposed of. The more deeply such lust becomes ingrained in our souls, the less free we are to enjoy the richer pleasures of communion, friendship, and self-giving love. Love and lust are no more compatible in the human heart than are generosity and greed.

Once we grasp this point, we can appreciate the way in which sin perverts desire. Every time we submit to evil we do nothing less than alter our tastes. This is the relevance of the

---

12. The great medieval theologian, Anselm, is quoted by various later theologians as saying, "If we should see the shame of sin on the one hand, and the pains of hell on the other, and must of necessity choose one; we would rather be thrust into hell without sin than to go into heaven with sin."

picture of Gollum preferring raw flesh to a cooked dinner. The reason sinful people do not delight in holy things is not because holy things are not incomparably better, but because all sin numbs our faculties. To yield to any form of evil is to convince oneself that bitter is sweet and sweet, bitter. The end result of such perversion is not men behaving like beasts, but men behaving like demons. Animals are known for sticking to their instincts. Demons are creatures that have turned their natures inside-out so that their existence is the opposite of its design. Such rewiring of the soul can only result in one experience: intense misery.

There is still more to say about the way in which holiness ought to change how we think about our existence. The willful rejection of holiness does not just pervert our appetites; it also defaces our moral beauty. Human beings have incredible dignity. According to the Bible, we are made in the image of God. This means that we were created to incarnate – that is to reveal and reflect – the hidden glory of God. Yet, the effect of sin is a deterioration of the soul such that, instead of being beautiful as God is beautiful, we distort the very nature of God into something that is grotesque and appalling. You need to know that, while a lot of sin may not alter your physical appearance, each sin does make the soul a little bit uglier. The human soul is just like the portrait of Dorian Gray. It records the damaging effect of every misdeed. This explains why standing in the light of holiness is such a painful experience. Exposed in this light, the mask of who we pretend to be is mercilessly stripped away. The profile is set before the face that it is intended to reflect. The soul is measured by nothing other than the immense perfection of God Himself. No human being can see the contrast between such excellence and deformity without being overwhelmed by a sense of ugliness and shame. The disparity between what we ought to be and what we are is just like Gollum having to confront his reflection in a mirror. The horror of such self-awareness can only result in one of two actions: either fleeing into the oblivion of darkness where truth can be ignored or spontaneously crying out, "God have mercy!"[13]

Of course, you may laugh at all of this and say that it has no grounding in fact. If so, my advice would be to pay closer attention to the testimony of conscience. The conscience is a unique human faculty which, more than any other part of the mind, gives testimony to the nature of deep moral truths. Yet, sadly, for many of us, the conscience has been placed under a strict gagging order. We've ignored its voice because we don't like what it has to say or how it makes us feel. Such spinelessness needs to be overcome if you are serious about making progress toward truth. There is no doubt that listening to our consciences may indeed result in condemning feelings of shame and guilt. But here, if we are patient, we may just find a positive lesson tucked away in a hurtful experience. There is the possibility that shame and guilt – rather than being just "negative emotions" – may in fact be deep intuitions about spiritual truth.[14] It just might be the case that, by paying attention to such signals, we are awakened from a paralyzing coma. Dare we even hope that such feelings may be the voice of wisdom calling us to abandon any pretense of goodness so that, left in abject humility, we begin to look out for help that we cannot find from within.

---

13. This truth makes sense of Peter's first experience of a miracle by Jesus. Rather than patting Jesus on the back or hollering in amazement, we read, "But when Simon Peter saw it, he fell down at Jesus' knees, saying, 'Depart from me, for I am a sinful man, O Lord'" (Luke 5:8).

14. James Davies in more than one book explores the ways in which negative emotions are often an insight that should be explored rather than suppressed. See *The Importance of Suffering: The Value and Meaning of Emotional Discontent* (New York: Routledge, 2011).

What If Justice Is Real?

Let's continue the effort to reimagine our existence. We can keep the image of Gollum exiting the cave, but add a fresh set of details to the scene. Let's now imagine that the world outside of the cave is not just a realm of greater light and life, but also a kingdom of perfect justice in which an inviolable standard of goodness and righteousness holds sway. The difference between Gollum's lair and the upper realm is the difference between anarchy and peace. Above, each crime receives its due punishment; below, anything goes so long as it is done in secret. The reason for this stark difference is that the ground above is ruled by a sovereign lord who boasts in justice and diligently seeks to uphold it. From time immemorial, he has governed a kingdom in which goodness is cherished and evil, condemned.

Now, recall the moral record of Gollum who has spent countless years practicing thievery and violence. His life is one big insult to the basic rules of civility and goodness. Of course, in doing such wickedness, he has always thought that his deeds were performed incognito. Yet, in this he was mistaken. For years, reports have spread of an evil creature who lives beneath the mountain in defiance of the edicts of the land and the jurisdiction of the king.

Using this extra information, let's reconstruct the scene when Gollum leaves the shadows of his den in order to rejoin the world of other creatures. If he were to saunter into the marketplace of a busy town, how do you think he would be received? Would the citizens welcome his presence? Would he be charitably embraced as a poor soul? Would they swipe past his reputation and act like nothing happened? Unlikely. Practical wisdom would warn everyone to treat Gollum like the outlaw that he is. He might be pitied, but he could not be trusted. His past guilt would follow him as closely as his shadow.

And what would the king do if it was reported that Gollum was spotted in a city square? Would he forget the names of the victims that Gollum left to rot underground? Would he allow a precedent to be set that a subject can live in rebellion against the law and face no consequences? This is even more unlikely. If the king were true to form, he would drag Gollum before a court of law, try him for his crimes, and punish him as a tribute to public justice. Any other scenario would be as detrimental to the character of the king as it would be to the welfare of the kingdom.

Now fast-forward the scene. Picture Gollum standing before a tribunal and offering his best attempt at what amounts to a defense. He is pleading that, although he has not been an upstanding member of the community, nevertheless, he is no worse than some other creatures such as orcs and trolls. He points out that there are plenty of other goblins under the mountain whose deeds color a darker resume than his own. He says that rules of the kingdom were not sufficiently promulgated – that, honest to God, no one told him that thievery and murder were capital offenses.

What do you think the king would say to such argumentation? Would it be admitted that orc-culture is a legitimate standard of goodness? Would the low bar of I-am-not-as-bad-as-others be a sufficient excuse for reprehensible behavior? Would purported ignorance justify repeated violations of innate rights and natural law? All such defenses would have no more weight before a good king than a pile of feathers. The standard of justice is not being better than the worst, but maintaining the given rules of a community; ignorance is never a warrant for crime, especially when a violation transgresses what ought to be recognized as a universal principle of morality; and not having touched rock bottom is an excuse so ludicrous that not even a teenager would attempt it. Therefore, on such a flimsy defense, Gollum would have no hope for a pardon. No righteous king would countenance clear and undeniable guilt. Such judicial blindness would not be merciful; it would be corrupt. The only options before the king would be (a) to degrade the majesty of the law or (b) to punish Gollum for his crimes.

Keeping all of this in view, we are now in a position to reflect on the relevance of this parable for you. The problem of sin is not just a subjective problem. In other words, the effect of sin is not merely that it limits the capacity of a sinner to enjoy what is good. The problem of sin is also relational; it involves God and the world that He has made. You must be made aware that the God of holiness is also the God of justice. This implies a further danger regarding sin that has not yet been mentioned. If God is unimpeachably righteous, He cannot be true to Himself, or maintain a reputation for justice, without condemning evil. To ignore guilt would be contrary to the dignity of His being and the health of His kingdom.[15]

You need to feel the tension of this point. Sinful human beings assume that God can make moral compromises because we imagine that He is like us, *imperfect*. But God is not a man, especially a sinful man. For God, a moral compromise is nothing less than a self-contradiction. As the sun emits light, so God emits justice. For God to overlook the least speck of moral guilt is a betrayal of all that He unchangeably is and all that He unchangeably loves.

It is only after we have confronted this truth that we can appreciate just how knotted the problem of human sin really is. Up until this point, you might imagine that you could hide out in "the cave" and ignore the realm of holiness. In

---

15. Men who struggle to make sense of this should read Paul's great letter to the Romans, especially chapters 1-8.

a secular context, we are habituated to think that religious truth is a subscription that one can opt into or opt out of. Yet, the presence of a holy and righteous God contradicts this mindset. Earth belongs to God no less than heaven. Although we may be able to lurk in the shadows of a depraved lifestyle for a season, the promise of God is that one day He will thoroughly search out and judge every perpetrator of evil from the ceiling of heaven to the basement of hell. This means that hiding from the eyes of justice is a futile strategy. You may be able to squat in the cave for a few decades, but eventually, like Gollum, a subpoena will arrive. You will find yourself standing before the grandest of kings having to give a defense for all of your deeds. According to the Bible, this court date is more certain than death itself.[16]

At this point, you may attempt to defend yourself with the argument that your sins are at worst misdemeanors. You may protest that Gollum is not a fair emblem of the moral quality of your life. However, you need to come to terms with two facts. The first is the reluctance of each one of us to be honest about the evil we have done. In truth, all of us have committed a lot more sins – and worse sins – than we are willing to confess. Here the testimony of conscience is damning. The self-talk of shame and guilt that each one of us endures regularly is compelling evidence that our hands are not nearly as clean as we would like others to believe.

Second, we need to be warned against using the adolescent plea of claiming innocence because there are other people worse than we are. Adults should not need to be taught the simple truth that guilt is not determined by a law of average,

---

16. Jesus repeatedly taught that He would return to judge the earth. This final judgment is basic to the apostolic message of the New Testament. Paul writes, "For we must all appear before the judgment seat of Christ, so that each one may receive what is due for what he has done in the body, whether good or evil" (2 Cor. 5:10).

but by a strict measure. A dad who finds money missing from his wallet does not ask his son, "Did any of your friends do this?" but, "Did you, or did you not, take money without asking?" Before the seat of judgment, the relevant question is never, "Am I good enough?" but, "Am I at fault?"

You need the courage to admit that, although you may not have committed every moral offense in the books, there is no shortage of sin in your life. Rather than cover your faults with the fig leaves of childish excuses, you need to own that Paul's stark assessment of the human race is not just true of humanity in general, but of *you* in particular. You, too, have sinned and fallen short of the glory of God (Rom. 3:23). Once this verdict is felt, there is a way in which the whole universe collapses in on itself. Everything that previously had such importance suddenly dissolves leaving a single state of affairs: me-before-God. In this position of extreme culpability, one thing matters and one thing alone. It's not the search for meaning; it's not the search for truth; it's not even the search for love. Everything stands or falls on the possibility of radical grace and undeserved mercy. The only question that has existential relevance when one steps out into the light of holiness is this: *Is there forgiveness for a sinner like me?*

This is the question we need to carry forward into the next chapter.

Shift the Gaze to Jesus

We've come a long way. The itinerary began with us waking up to the reality of being in a cave. At first, we thought that a few questions were the only tonic needed to escape the inauthenticity of the herd. Yet, the appearance of the cave exposed a staggering degree of human darkness. We are not just out of touch with ourselves; we are out of touch with reality.

It seemed, for a while at least, that salvation could come through enlightenment. Truth itself might have the potency needed to release us from our bondage. But, such optimism dissolved after a closer inspection of our moral condition. We learned that we are in the cave not just because we are ignorant, but because we are hiding. Lost, mistaken, and confused, we are also guilty, defiled, and rebellious. The core problem of the cave is the inherent conflict between sin and holiness. We cannot step out into the light of holiness without that very same light convicting and threatening us. Left naked in sin, human beings are no more able to stand safely in the presence of God than we can stand safely on the surface of the sun.

It was only by stubbing our toes against these truths that we fully awakened to what it means to exist in the cave. To use the language of the Old Testament, the cave is not just a condition; it's a curse. We are living in a kind of outer darkness that is sealed off from the fullness of life, which is both the source and end of our existence. Cut off from God, we are cut off from the waters of joy.

It's important to recognise that this plight is not the penalty of a few, but the universal condition of man *left to himself.* This means that the very people we might look to for help to rescue us from the cave – the Platos, the Buddhas, and the Einsteins – all of them are trapped in the same position. Thus, from a purely human point of view, the situation is indeed hopeless. Technology can make us a bit more comfortable and amused while wasting away in the dark, but it cannot free us. Likewise, psychology can soothe some of our negative emotions and explain hidden aspects of our misery, but it cannot provide atonement. We are collectively in the most damning of circumstances. No act of penance can pay off the debt of our transgressions. Equally, death itself is not an escape from the claims of divine justice. All we can do is distract ourselves nervously while we await a day in which we will be summoned, individually, to explain the courses of our lives.

So, here we find our place in the present journey. We are stuck in the cave in a rising tide of despair and gloom. We cannot return to the oblivion of the crowd. We know too much to be happy there. Neither can we move forward. The barrier of sin is too great for the abilities of the self. What, then, can be done?

As is often the case, crises are not just moments of confusion, but of sobriety. Here, on the brink of despair, at a moment when the soul is sliding toward uncertainty, the voice of Wisdom speaks again to those with ears to hear. What she says is a shaft of light and a word of hope. Softly, she tells you that it's time to stop looking at yourself and time to turn your eyes onto Jesus.

Shifting the Attention

It's time to flip the script of what we have been doing thus far. Up until now, there has been an assumption at work that may have gone unnoticed. This may have been invisible to you due to its prevalence in modern thinking. So far, the book has been built on a "how" question, namely, "How can I find a better life?" The focus, in other words, has been on "me," the subject, and on my personal aptitude to find a method or program by which I can improve my existence (i.e., exit the cave). It's time now to abandon this mindset and adopt a new framework of thinking. We need to shift, that is, from a "how" question to a "who" question. Given the fact that we've bumped into a wall of hopelessness, that we *personally* cannot do anything to change our spiritual circumstances, we need now to lift our eyes off of ourselves and investigate whether – if there is no hope in the self – there may be hope from elsewhere.

This shift is important for two reasons. First, it marks the conception of humility. For as long as I look to myself to fix my own problems, whether consciously or not, I am operating on the basis of a vain confidence that used to be labeled "spiritual pride." All of the great doctors of the soul have noted the same danger regarding pride: It is the chief barrier restricting any form of spiritual growth.[1] To break out of this attitude and to succumb to humility is nothing less than a revolution of the heart. It is a softening of granite into clay.

---

1. Humility is a deeply misunderstood virtue. A helpful introduction is *Humility* by Andrew Murray (Essential Christian Classics, 2014).

Second, the shift from "how" to "who" transitions us from thinking in terms of self-improvement to thinking in terms of salvation. It should be evident by now that the only hope we have to exit the cave is the availability of an extrinsic power, the presence of someone who is untouched by the domain of sin and death. Here I am reminded of Moses' farewell remarks to the Israelites. Before ascending up Mount Pisgah, he tells them that the wisdom needed as they cross the Jordan is not hidden in the heavens or kept across the sea in some unattainable place. Instead, he says, "The word is very near you. It is in your mouth and in your heart" (Deuteronomy 30:14). So it is in the modern world. The marvel of living in a post-Christian civilization is that the truth needed to guide us is already at our fingertips.[2] Anyone who has sung a carol like "Hark the Herald" or "Joy to the World" has the basic information needed to find a thread to get out of the cave. The "who" we are searching for is not a scientist, philosopher, or mystic yet to be unveiled. It is a Jewish carpenter whom billions already adore. Therefore, the great challenge before us is not to describe something new, but to recover something forgotten. We must excavate the past and try to understand why, even in the twilight of modernity, Jesus is nothing less than the light of the world.

Now, I am fully aware that a lot of men will balk at any reference to Jesus. You need to understand one thing about such a knee-jerk reaction. It is based on prejudice, not reason. Rare is the man who has thought carefully about the claims of Christianity and rejected them on the basis of independent

---

2. At the start of *Orthodoxy*, Chesterton writes, "I have often had a fancy for writing a romance about an English yachtsman who slightly miscalculated his course and discovered England under the impression that it was a new island in the South Seas" (Kindle edition). This is the experience of men discovering Christianity today. It's always been there; it's just never been appreciated.

judgment. If you are put off by the mention of Jesus, more than likely the cause is unfiltered bias. Once more, you have stumbled into a herd mentality. If inspired by nothing nobler than curiosity, you owe it to yourself at least once in your lifetime to investigate the truth claims of Jesus. In a best-case scenario, you will experience for yourself what Jesus refers to as abundant life. In a worst-case scenario, you will formulate personal convictions and exercise independent thinking. In no case at all will time and energy have been wasted.

Recovering the Unique Identity of Jesus

There are any number of ways that we could approach the subject-matter of Jesus. I'm going to take a shortcut to keep pace. Rather than piece together a profile of Jesus one New Testament quotation at a time, I am going to assume the classic understanding of Jesus shared by Christians across a vast spectrum of churches – Protestant, Roman Catholic, and Orthodox. Such an approach may sound strange to some, even suspicious. However, there are solid rational grounds for doing this. The complete form of Jesus generates a compelling proof when it is set beside the existential needs of the soul. We can liken this proof to a key that is needed to open a locked door.

Picture a door that is locked shut. A crowd of philosophers is standing next to the door puzzling over the cause of the predicament. Beside them is a group of scientists who are taking measurements of the doorframe and engineering a device to cut through the barrier irrespective of its form and significance. What both groups overlook is a table nearby with a key on it. If this key were picked up and used, everyone in the room would soon discover that the door could swing open with a mere twist of the wrist. But, there the key lies unnoticed, gathering dust.

The meaning of the illustration is this: suitability and effectiveness are two compelling forms of evidence. When two things match as closely as the teeth of a key and the pins of a lock, there is good reason to ponder whether the one object exists for the sake of the other. Likewise, when a tool is effective in resolving an otherwise intractable problem, there is just cause to take it up and use it in its given form.[3]

This insight helps us understand why the orthodox understanding of Jesus should be taken as is, rather than pieced together like a jigsaw puzzle. One of the great evidences of the truthfulness of Jesus is the suitability of His person to our needs. The more we study Him, the more we marvel at the degree to which His identity and mission meet the requirements of our moral and spiritual needs. The fit is no less exact than a key in a lock. This by itself is amazing. But, what is equally astounding is the potency of Jesus. Countless people have discovered through the ages that Jesus is able to do for them something that cannot be replicated otherwise – either through philosophy or science. What this is precisely is something that we are not yet ready to discuss. First things first. Need number one is to gain some understanding of the uniqueness of Jesus' person.[4]

Our method for doing this will be to identify and refute some of the most common misconceptions about Jesus. Sculptors reveal the hidden form of a statue by chipping away unwanted pieces of stone. Similarly, for us, it will be by discrediting protuberant ideas that the beauty of Jesus' form is progressively unveiled.

---

3. The suitability of the gospel to the moral needs of man is an argument that Thomas Chalmers takes up in his *Institutes of Theology* and elsewhere.

4. Men interested in an overview of this topic, see Donald Macleod, *The Person of Christ* (IVP, 1998).

Is Jesus an Avatar?

Repeatedly through history some people have pictured Jesus to be truly God, but not truly man. This belief was a particular temptation in the ancient world for people who were accustomed to stories of Zeus and of other gods visiting human society, often for the sake of a one-night stand. It's not hard to see the facile similarity between these stories and the gospel history in which the Son of God assumes flesh and is born as Jesus. Yet, the similarity is a mirage. In Greek myths, there is no true union of God and man when Zeus decides to go for a romp in the hay. Zeus uses human nature more or less as an avatar. He changes his form without adopting a new nature. In fact, we can say more than this: An incarnation – in the Christian sense – was inconceivable within the framework of Greek thinking.[5] Zeus could no more take on the nature of a man than a man could take on the nature of a cat. There were two barriers that made such an event impossible: one was the pride of Zeus; the other was the inherent contradiction between divine and human nature. The infinite and finite coexisting in a single person? Plato would not be able to withhold his laughter at the suggestion.

Nevertheless, such humility – and such mystery – is precisely what Christians adore in the person of Jesus. They recognise that Jesus is not God crossdressing as a man for the sake of a novel experience. Jesus is God-in-flesh, Immanuel. Cut His skin and you can paradoxically say that

---

5. People often assume that stories about pagan gods being born as people are parallels to the gospel. They are not. In such stories gods are either born in mythic time, which is to say, out of time, or they are given no preexistence. Hercules became a god; he was not one before he was born. No pagan god would degrade his majesty by assuming a human nature.

God is bleeding. His mother was just as human as anyone else born in Bethlehem. He was like us in all things with a single exception: He had no propensity to sin.[6]

Is Jesus an Activist?

Equally mistaken is the idea that Jesus is 100% human, but – *that is all*. This is the typical mindset of academic historians, the kind of people who get interviewed in documentaries for television networks. Listen to the subtexts and they speak of Jesus as being no different from Confucius, Buddha, Muhammed, or any other historical figure of influence. They refer to Him as being a lot of things – an inspired prophet, a religious founder, a political revolutionary, a victim of social injustice. But there is one thing He is most certainly not: *God*. Their worldview can no more conceive of an incarnation than could that of the ancient Greeks. Close-minded to the prospect of mystery, they cut Jesus down in size until He is small enough to fit the tiny cubbyholes of a materialistic worldview.

This mindset is just as wrong as the previous one. The claim throughout the New Testament is not that Jesus is a mere prophet. Prophets were special, but not unique. Nor was He a mere teacher, reformer, or miracle worker. Such men came and went. The revelation at the heart of the New Testament is that Jesus is to history what the sun is to our solar system. Although He is a human being like us, He is also a human being unlike us. Jesus is the only object in creation that can be given the honor, acclaim, and devotion that belongs to immortal God without breaking the sacred

---

6. Marilynne Robinson says, "There is much that is thrilling and telling in the thought that true divinity can assume the place of a human being and yet remain an ordinary man to every mortal eye." See *The Givenness of Things: Essays* (Virago Press, 2015).

prohibition against idolatry.[7] Why is this? The answer is as simple as it is scandalous: Jesus is God. His mother was a human being just like ours. His father, not so; His Father was Uncreated Power.

Is Jesus a Superhero?

A third mistake is to try to balance the proportions of Jesus. Here we might imagine that Jesus is a demi-god, a cross breed between something heavenly and earthly. The recipe may be 50/50, 80/20, or 40/60. The precise makeup does not matter so long as the end result adds up to 100.

Such thinking is not new. The ancient world was littered with stories of superhumans like Achilles and Theseus who were products of split parentage. The end result of such unions was a hybrid child with otherworldly strength, beauty, and abilities – heroes worthy of a lead role in a Marvel film.[8]

More than once, a clever religious teacher has tried to understand Jesus in such terms. In some cultural settings, the message of the gospel is more palatable if Jesus is pictured as somewhere between God and man on the chain of being rather than a union of God and man in a single person. There is something about the logic of Jesus having two complete natures that short-circuits the human intellect. Unable to do the math, we feel the need to readjust the formula.

Yet, the incarnation is nothing if not mind boggling. The mystery of the person of Christ is that, when you look at Him, you are not seeing a watered-down version of God or a souped-up version of man. Rather, you are beholding the

---

7. The historian and New Testament scholar Richard Bauckham is excellent on the topic of demonstrating Jesus' divine identity. See *Jesus and the God of Israel* (Eerdmans, 2008).

8. This was the famous Arian heresy of the early church. The great theologian who tirelessly worked to expose it was Athanasius. His classic *On the Incarnation* (Icthus Publications, 2018) is essential reading.

perfect image of both at once. Jesus expresses uncorrupted holiness while equally expressing unadulterated humanity. He is the unique God-man, one person with two natures that coexist without confusion, without change, without division, and without separation.[9]

If this sounds confusing, that's okay. The deepest truths of the universe are not riddles to be solved but mysteries to be adored. Not many men feel a compulsion to dismiss science if they fail to comprehend the densest intricacies of quantum physics or molecular biology. We are humble enough to admit that some truths are above our paygrade. We need to demonstrate the same humility when it comes to theology. If the universe is too complicated for our understanding – and if God is incomparably greater than the universe – then we ought to expect to hit a depth beyond our mental reach. Jesus is not just a mystery among others. Next to the Trinity, He is the greatest mystery of all.[10]

Yet, acknowledging this limit should not pull the plug on our thinking. Instead, it should redirect the current of our interests in a new direction. Although very little has been revealed about the metaphysical composition of Jesus, His missional significance is the main theme of the Bible. It is to this latter topic that we now need to turn our attention. The question, "*Why* did the incarnation happen?" is of far greater relevance than the question, "*How* did the incarnation happen?" To contemplate the second one is interesting, but unimportant. To ponder the first one is to pick up the thread of the last chapter and to follow it in the direction of wisdom and grace.

---

9. The language in the sentence comes from The Chalcedonian Creed.
10. The great hymn-writer, Isaac Watts, says, "Where reason fails with all her power, there faith prevails, and love adores."

The Relevance of the Incarnation for Guys in the Cave

A lot of surprising things have been discovered under the sheets of history. Lost civilisations have been found; famous documents have been exposed as frauds; prehistoric animals have been dug up and showcased. History is full of unanticipated revelations. However, one event towers above all the rest as the least likely of possibilities. This is the birth of God as a man. To pause and reflect that such an event happened ought to excite our interest intolerably. If the incarnation is true, it is not one page among others in the big book of history; it is nothing less than the light of the world visiting earth as a man. All of our greatest questions – those of origin, purpose, and design – take on fresh meaning in the light of this extraordinary event. This is why no level-headed person can be incurious about Jesus. Discovering Jesus is like finding a lost key to a safe that could not previously be opened. Suddenly, the unsearchable will of God is made plain.

There is an implication of this that you should not miss: caring about Jesus is ultimately the same as caring about oneself. Our happiness is determined not just by physical and psychological principles. More fundamentally, Jesus reveals our place in the universe.

How precisely is this the case? The answer can be broken down into the following five points.

Jesus Came to Do for Us What We Could Not Do for Ourselves

Picture a society in which every aspect of life is broken and entangled in a vast system of corruption caused by the prevalence of harmful narcotics. Every single member of the society is an addict, to one degree or another. The entire economy is based on profiting from the trading and selling of these substances. Politics is absorbed in protecting the interests of the drug manufacturers and the users. This is Gotham City, only without the presence of a heroic journalist, a renegade police chief, and Batman.

Now, ask the question: how could anyone living in such a place be rescued from the poisonous effects of drugs? If everyone is implicated in the problem, who will provide a solution? Help cannot come from within the system. The reason for this is plain: no one on the inside has the innocence and freedom needed to bring about change. If there is to be help, help must come from the outside. Someone must exist who is untouched by addiction and uninfluenced by corruption. But more must be the case. Such a person must be willing to enter into the brokenness of a perverse society in order to bring about salvation from the inside. Unless these conditions are met, the errant society will be trapped in a vicious whirlpool of depravity. Without a savior, there will be no salvation.

This image can help us understand the logic behind the incarnation. The problem of sin is the greatest systemic problem of all. The Apostle Paul gives an incisive account of this in his letter to the Romans. He demonstrates mercilessly that no one is free from the problem of sin. All are "under sin" (Rom. 3:9) – not just in the sense that we are guilty, but in the sense that we are enslaved. We are no more able to liberate ourselves from our destructive appetites than a lifelong drug addict (nestled in a society built on drug use) will be able to come clean.

The wonder of the incarnation is that someone from the outside has indeed come into our world. Moreover, that someone – a person we have now identified as the very Son of God – is untainted by evil appetites, moral weakness, or peer pressure. He can bring us hope precisely because He is both innocent and powerful. Where we fail due to weakness, He perseveres in righteousness; where we succumb to temptation, He conquers evil with good. This is the good news of the incarnation. Jesus is God entering into our world in order to do for us what we could never get done for ourselves. In Jesus, God demonstrates that He is unwilling to be a detached spectator of our suffering. Jesus is God's might entering the world in order to fix our greatest problem – not from the outside – but from the inside.[11]

Jesus Came to Teach Us What We Could Not Discover Otherwise

There are essentially three paths available to human beings as we try to figure out our origin, purpose, and design. One is **mysticism**. This is the action of closing our eyes, detaching from the world, and trying to find truth inside of ourselves. The appeal of mysticism is the depth of the human soul. Human beings have undeniable interiority. We are a spiritual onion that hides multiple layers of selfhood beneath the flaky skin of existence.

Yet, as fascinating as self-analysis is, this act is fraught with danger. In terms of the effort to discover truth, the inward eye is prone to self-deception. Marx, Nietzsche, and Freud have each in their own way highlighted something that is equally discernible by reading the Old Testament prophets – namely, the duplicity of the human heart. To look inwardly is not to see truth through a clear window; it is to feel lost in a house of mirrors. The end result is disorientation, not enlightenment. The more we navel-gaze the less attached we feel to any stable structure of reality.

---

11. In *Mere Christianity*, C.S. Lewis says, "Christianity is the story of how the rightful king has landed, you might say landed in disguise, and is calling us to take part in his great campaign of sabotage" (Macmillan, 1956).

The second path is **science**. Here we turn outward to the material universe to find answers to our existential questions. The benefits of doing so have been demonstrated prolifically by the discoveries and innovations made through scientific research over the last three centuries. Who would want to live without modern science? Thirty minutes with the dentist is ample proof that some things in the world have improved since the toothache of our ancestors.

Nonetheless, the great novelist Marilynne Robinson hits the nail on the head when she speaks of human beings as living in a cocoon. There is no logical reason to believe that the majority of truth, much less the most important truth, is accessible to human beings through our senses. Our presence in the universe is like that of a bug in a garden. Sight, smell, taste, hearing and touch – plus a puny intellect – are a meager toolkit for investigating the full dimensions of the environment around us. Our problem is not just what we *do not* know, but what we *cannot* know. Like a child holding an empty cup to an unreachable faucet, humanity looks to stars for unattainable answers.[12]

The **incarnation** provides a third means of apprehending truth. Without denying the mysterious depths of the soul or the productiveness of science, the incarnation manifests that God has spoken to us in a way that is more direct and personal through the gift of His Son. Jesus is not just a rescuer from an outside realm; He is also a herald from an outside realm. He is able to tell us things about the nature of God, the will of God, the design of man, and the end of man – things that are otherwise unsearchable. This is part of what John, the gospel writer, means when he labels Jesus first "the Word" and

---

12. A helpful way to recover the complexity of reality is to read *An Immense World: How Animal Senses Reveal the World around Us* by Ed Yong (Vintage, 2023).

later "the Word made flesh." The entirety of Jesus' existence is revelatory. His actions as well as His teaching are nothing less than a mode of communication between God and man.

This point is of particular interest given the predicament of the cave. If there is a way out of the cave, Jesus is uniquely positioned to know about it. Unlike the rest of us, His existence did not begin in the darkness, but in the light. He came from the outside *in*. This means that He is in a unique position to help those stuck inside find a way out.[13]

Jesus Came to Beautify Holiness

No concept related to God is more important than holiness. Holiness refers not just to things that are related to God, but to things that are intrinsic to God. God is preeminently the Holy One. His character and being are fundamentally holy.

Up to this point, we have exclusively thought about holiness in terms of justice, truth, and purity. Holiness is what inhibits sinners from existing in safe proximity with God. We are confined to the cave because we are unholy – that is to say, defiled by moral guilt and subject to divine judgment.

The incarnation reveals that this picture, though true, is incomplete. Holiness is a complex thing like a mountain, which can be viewed from multiple perspectives. The human mind has a similar problem regarding holiness that the eye has when observing gigantic three-dimensional objects. We can only see one angle at a time. Just as there is no one position from which a person can view the whole of Mount Kilimanjaro, likewise, holiness can never be apprehended by any single concept. Holiness is as infinitely fascinating as God Himself.

---

13. It's noteworthy how many times Jesus speaks of being "sent." He is insistent that people recognize Him as a unique communication from the Father.

Now, Jesus, the God-man, brings into relief a facet of holiness that we have not yet mentioned. This is the grace, mercy, and love of God. What we discover through observing Jesus is that love is every bit as intrinsic to holiness as is justice. The God who gives the Ten Commandments is also the God who comes as a baby to be the Savior of the world. One peak is not greater than the other: justice and mercy fill the same volume in the heart of God.

Recognising this ought to heighten our appreciation of Jesus. Jesus is not just a good man healing lepers and feeding the hungry from a spirit of pity. Jesus is the holiness of God expressing itself through acts of grace and love.[14] This leads us to an insight that may, at first, sound paradoxical. Somehow, holiness is both the justice of God that threatens sinners and the love of God that seeks after them. How this tension can be resolved is the subject matter of the next chapter. The point not to miss here is the degree to which we depend on Jesus to have a more complete understanding of what it means that God is holy.[15]

Jesus Came to Reiterate the Dignity of Man

One of the shocking revelations of the incarnation is that God *could* join His nature to that of a human being. This possibility should not be taken for granted. There is no reason to suppose that God could take the form of a tiger, or a mole, or an eagle and use them to express His being. The nature of these animals is incompatible with the nature of God. Animals, as amazing

---

14. The ever-poetic theologian Thomas Watson says, "Christ took our flesh in order that he might make our human nature lovely to God and the divine nature appear lovely to man." See *A Body of Divinity* (Kindle edition).

15. John's gospel puts the matter this way: "For the law was given through Moses; grace and truth came through Jesus Christ. No one has ever seen God; the only God, who is at the Father's side, he has made him known" (1:17-18).

as they are, lack the freedom, will, intellect, and imagination needed to reflect personal existence.[16]

Not so with human beings. The incarnation reiterates for us that, when the Bible says we were made in the image of God (cf. Genesis 1:27), it means exactly what it says. Our nature, as hard to believe as it may sound, is able to bear something of the weight of divine glory. God is able to take the form of a man because man is able, by design, to reflect the life of God. Marilynne Robinson captures this truth when she says, "Jesus is the profoundest praise of humankind the cosmos could utter."[17] Her point is that the incarnation is not just a statement about God; it's also a statement about man. In Jesus, we see the flower of our nature. We see beyond the sordidness of our fallen condition to the heights of our moral and spiritual capacities. Human beings were designed for nothing less than communicating holiness. And this is precisely what the human nature of Jesus does. His humanity is a translucent veil through which God is seen. That God could attain so much through the raw material of humanity ought to inspire us to reevaluate two things. One is the evil of sin; the other is the dignity of man.

Jesus Came to Define Authenticity

Our culture loves to talk about authenticity. We all want a "true" existence. Our problem is that we lack any clear definition of what authenticity is.

A final relevance of the incarnation is that, in Jesus, we see what it means to be fully alive. When Christians say that Jesus was without sin, we mean that, in Him, there was nothing off target, no stepping over boundaries, nothing twisted or corrupt on the inside. He has no basis for shame

---

16. This is one of many reasons why the Israelites were warned so adamantly not to make idols.

17. See Robinson, *The Givenness of Things:* (Virago Press, 2015).

or guilt. He was free in the most important sense of the word: There was no downward gravity to bind or frustrate His will from fulfilling its deepest purpose of loving and glorifying God. For this reason, the life of Jesus was more fulfilling than that of any other human being. Joy, peace, and righteousness flowed frictionless through His heart.

One implication of this is that Jesus is uniquely able to provide a model of authenticity for the rest of us. If we want to know what it means to be fully alive as a human being, or to achieve liberty, the best place to look is the example of the God-man. He alone is perfect, not just in His divinity, but in His humanity. This means that He alone is able to show us the highest form of life which our nature can attain.

What, then, do we discover when we observe Jesus? His life is in many ways the opposite of what we might expect. We don't see independence. We don't see self-reliance. We don't see self-esteem. We don't see self-assertion. Instead, we see a human will fully yielded to the will of God. What we find in Jesus is the following spiritual principle: We are most ourselves, not when we resist God, or pretend to be God, but when we submit most fully to God.[18] Authenticity, in other words, is obedience, especially that obedience whereby I give up my "rights" in order to love someone else.

Keeping to the Trail

Much has been said about Jesus. The need now is to connect these truths back to the fundamental problem of the cave. What we discover through studying the incarnation is that God Himself is unhappy with our predicament. More than we want freedom and joy for ourselves, He desires these things for us. In fact, the love of God is so great that He sent His beloved Son into our world as a Savior for sinners. This

---

18. This is inspired by a statement Bishop Barron made during a Christmas homily.

is good news. The incarnation is a bright flare that indicates help is on the way. Holiness may be against us, but it is also for us. The justice of God cannot outpace the mercy of God.

Yet, latent within this hope is a tension that has not yet been resolved. Up until now, justice and mercy appear to be irreconcilable. God cannot be both righteous and gracious at the same time. Either sin will be condemned, which means the death of sinners, or sin will be ignored, which means the death of justice. No third way has yet been found by which mercy and justice can be honored simultaneously.

It is caught on the horns of this dilemma that we need to move on to the next stage of our journey. The incarnation tells us that a rescuer has entered the cave; but the incarnation does not itself indicate what form the rescue will take. To find an answer to this new question we must advance from the mystery of the incarnation to the mystery of the cross.

Feel the Weight of the Cross

There is one act of self-restraint that must be maintained right now: We must keep our eyes off of the self. This is easier said than done. The self is like a speck of dust in the eye; it irritatingly absorbs all attention, inhibiting us from catching sight of the bigger, more important truths beyond us.

Now, the truth we need to keep our eyes glued onto is that of Jesus. Eventually, we will get back to the question of how to exit the cave. To do so will require further self-analysis. However, we are not yet ready for this. Until a more solid foundation is laid regarding the significance of Jesus, we can no more enjoy freedom than we can float in thin air.

As we continue to reflect on Jesus, it is important to think of Him not as "my truth," or "your truth," or "one mode of truth," but as *the truth*. One of the devious myths of the modern world is that different truths exist for different people. We especially think this way when the topic under discussion is that of religion. Whereas the facts of physics and chemistry are perceived to be hard and incontrovertible, the stuff of religion is often assumed to be plastic. Modern people tend *not* to think of faith as interacting with things that are real, permanent, and universally relevant. Rather, religious truths are like pieces of clothing that can be tried on, put off, and exchanged – all according to no criteria more important than that of fancy or fashion. So long as a person's religion "works for him," that's all that matters. Dipping into Buddhism, Christianity, or a touch of Islam is not much different than deciding whether to grow a beard or shave one.

For the sake of our souls, we need to shed this mode of thinking. Truth is *truth* regardless of the topic – morality or gravity. A person no more gets to pick the fundamental articles of religion than he gets to choose which elements to put on the Periodic Table. Jesus Himself was clear on this point. He did not walk the streets of Jerusalem peddling Himself as one option among multiple rabbis. Rather, without a hint of irony, He said, "I am the way, the truth, and the life" (John 14:6). Elsewhere, He unflinchingly called Himself "the light of the world." These claims are astonishing. In using the metaphor of light, Jesus is saying that He is to the human soul what the sun is to the earth. We depend on Him absolutely for light and life. With Him, we see; we live. Without Him, we are blind; we are not just dying, we are *dead*.

This understood, we can move on and pick up the thread from the last chapter. So far, all we have learned about Jesus is that His identity is unique. He is 100% man and 100% God. This strange identity (and it is indeed strange) begs a question that has been danced around but not picked up directly. It is this: Why did Jesus come? We've briefly said that He was on a rescue mission. What has not yet been stated is the nature of the rescue. Nothing has been communicated about how Jesus factors into the dismal equation of sin + holiness = condemnation and punishment.

Many will have some familiarity with the idea that Jesus died on a cross. But, for a lot of guys, this idea will be fuzzy and ill-defined. There will be a dangerous risk of lumping Jesus together with other well-meaning figures who suffered and died for noble causes. In the annals of history, it's not hard to find examples of good men who were unjustly punished due to the eccentricity of their character (e.g., Socrates), their cause (e.g., Tyndale), or their message (e.g., Galileo). It's tempting to think of Jesus as one such figure – a great man whose greatness appeared too early on the stage of history to be noticed and appreciated. Yet, to file Jesus in any class of people – regardless of how stellar the class may be – is to make a category mistake. Jesus is unique in the true sense of the word (not "special" but "one of a kind"). Many great men have been put to death; only Jesus was born to die. Many heroes have demonstrated courage in the face of excruciating pain; only Jesus drained the curse of God until the cup was without a drop remaining.

This may sound confusing. That's okay. The rest of this chapter will explain the import of Jesus' death. What matters now is keeping the gaze on Jesus and off the self. It will only be by looking at Jesus, and more specifically at the cross, that we understand the relevance of the profound words, "When you have lifted up the Son of Man, then you will know that I am he" (John 8:28).

Overcoming the Modern Prejudice Against Religion

Broadly, humankind has two sets of spiritual intuitions. One is that the world is rationally ordered. We look to the heavens, marvel at the elegant beauty of the stars and night sky, and feel prompted to search for some invisible structure framing our existence. Such are the conditions in which philosophy is conceived.

119

The other set of intuitions might be called religious. These are stranger and more foreign to a lot of Western people. They include the feelings that there is something sacred in the order of being; that sacrilege is an existential danger; that sacrifice is essential for making contact – and keeping up positive relations – with a transcendental center of power; and that some mysteries defy the childish algorithm of human reason. Countless philosophers and scientists have mocked such intuitions, often through the patronizing attempt to reduce them to evolutionary needs. Yet, the testimony among human beings is too broad and too ancient to cancel. Man is not just homo sapiens. He is also homo adorans. Religious awe is as deeply imprinted into the soul of man as is the principle of reason.[1]

Among these impressions, there is one that needs to be highlighted. This is the felt need for sacrifice. From the point of view of the Bible, indigenous religions are fundamentally wrong in terms of how they perform sacrifices and how they understand them. Yet, in the midst of flagrant cultural errors, primitive religions get a few things right that are glaringly absent from the cult of modern life.[2] These include a subliminal source of shame, a dread of imminent wrath, and a liturgical respect for the potency of blood. In this sense, it is no exaggeration to say that the ancient Egyptians and Aztecs were closer to some dimensions of truth than are modern Brits and Americans. The first group at least understood that there was an intersection of sacredness and truth. They understood that man's needs were not first biological and then religious; they were first religious and then biological.

---

1. This is one of many profound themes in C.S. Lewis's story, *Till We Have Faces* (HarperCollins, 1978).

2. To recover this insight see Timothy Larson, *The Slain God: Anthropologists and the Christian Faith* (Oxford University Press, 2014).

Modern men need to reflect on this. We live in a materialistic world that whitewashes over our religious instincts and numbs our spiritual yearnings. If one half of the soul is telling us to think more deeply about the order of the universe around us (i.e., pursue philosophy), the other half is crying out for us to take off our shoes and acknowledge that we are walking on holy ground (i.e., pursue religion). These two halves of the soul need not be put in competition with each other. In fact, one of the most compelling proofs of Christianity is the degree to which it speaks to all of the needs and interests of the human person. In the Christian faith, wisdom and reverence lead us to the same centerpoint of reality: The mind that encodes the universe with order is also the voice that says, "I am."

Paying attention to these intuitions prepares the mind for contemplating the death of Jesus. Throughout the New Testament, the governing concept for understanding the cross is that of a sacrifice. Jesus is not most importantly a hero, or a martyr, or a prophet. He is a lamb who takes away the sins of the world. In His death we discover the true form of all that man has vainly attempted through errant religions. We find, in other words, a way of balancing sin and holiness so that, instead of resulting in condemnation and death, it equals forgiveness and life. This is the unique power of the cross which has been celebrated and remembered through countless Christian hymns and liturgies through the ages.

Surveying the Wondrous Cross

Understanding the cross is like trying to draw a map of the universe. There will always be more than can fit on a page – or in books, or even in libraries. Therefore, from the outset, it is important to limit our focus according to what is achievable and what is of first importance. For us, this is the significance of the cross in terms of justice and holiness. These, you may remember, are the factors that generate the problem of the cave. Our job now is to find a solution to the problem.

To begin, we need to distinguish between justice and holiness.[3] To do so, it is helpful to picture two circles, one smaller within one larger. This illustrates the way in which these concepts are related, but not identical. Justice is merely one part of holiness; holiness is a bigger reality.

More specifically, justice, on the one hand, refers to God's commitment to render to each human act its due reward. God will ensure that the moral fabric of the universe is maintained. He will act in such a way that the connection between evil and punishment and goodness and blessing is upheld and honored. He will do this precisely because He is just. Such is His character.

Holiness, on the other hand, refers most importantly not to God's treatment of sin and righteousness, but to His *attitude* toward both. God *in His being* cherishes what is good and hates what is evil. God does not just judge sin; He is the opposite of sin in the sense of being opposed to sin and actively committed to destroying it. Sin can no more dwell in the presence of God than malice can dwell in a heart of love, greed in generosity, cruelty in mercy, or pride in humility. To God, sin is not just detestable for what it results in; it is abominable for what it is. Sin is a pollutant that must either be cleansed and eradicated or publicly exposed and vilified. Under no terms can God tolerate sin. To do so would be nothing less than the death of God Himself. There is simply no space in the created order for God to be all-in-all and for sin to be left alone.

---

3. Jonathan Edwards is particularly helpful on this point. See his essay "Satisfaction for Sin" in *Miscellanies* (Yale University Press, 2002).

Appreciating this distinction is important for one main reason: it demonstrates the need to look at the cross from two complementary points of view. We must first set it against the backdrop of justice; we must then go on and do the same for holiness. It will only be after having appreciated it in both frameworks that we will understand just how important the cross is for the religious needs of man.

The Need for Justice to Be Satisfied

One of the primary metaphors for sin in the Bible is that of debt.[4] The image teaches us that every moral infraction results in an imbalance of justice. This imbalance must be rectified or else penalties will ensue. Any child who has ever experienced righteous discipline is aware of this dynamic. A parent cannot blithely forgive a purposeful violation of a household rule. There are times when punishment must be meted out. This is why Lady Justice is so often pictured as having scales in one hand and a sword in the other. To overlook some faults is not an act of mercy; it's a violation of righteousness.

This point needs to be crystal clear in the mind of each reader. To make sure this happens, let me offer an extended illustration.

Picture a man (we'll name him "Steve") who brazenly defies the speed limits of a highway code. Naively, Steve does so thinking that no one is observing his offenses and that he is getting away with his behavior scot-free. What Steve doesn't realize is that hidden cameras are clocking his speeding and that an online database is keeping a tally. Sometime in the future, the moral indifference of Steve is going to be disrupted when an unexpected bill comes through the mail.

---

4. Gary Anderson explores the relevant Biblical material behind the metaphor in *Sin: A History* (New Haven: Yale, 2010).

By fine or by punishment, he will soon find out that a moral debt to society has been incurred, one that must be paid off.

Now, in using the imagery of debt for sin, the Bible is informing us that sin does indeed have consequences. When we break a moral law, we often feel as if we do so without contracting any liabilities. After all, the secular world is set up to make us feel as if no divine eye is monitoring our affairs. Yet, to think this is naive. Not only is there a God, but *the-God-who-is* is just. Each sin is a violation of three things: His righteous character, His righteous laws, and the righteous fabric of His kingdom. Such trespasses cannot be ignored. For God to wink at sin would be gross negligence, a dereliction of duty. It would give cause for men and women to protest that God is unworthy of the seat He fills. Thus, justice itself demands that God notice, record, and, at some point, bring to account all acts of evil. Only through this process can God's name be vindicated, the goodness of the world kept intact, and the scales of justice balanced.[5]

But there is more that we can learn from the illustration.

In the story, Steve did not commit one offense, but many. It's worth pausing to think about this fact. Common sense teaches that every additional violation increases the penalty needed to restore the order of justice. We see this principle operating in society on a daily basis. The more speeding tickets someone receives, the greater penalty needed to cancel the summary debt. Even a child would recognize that it would be unfair for a man who has been caught speeding 100 times to be treated the same as a man caught only once. The demerit of the first man is greater than that of the second and, accordingly, the first man ought to pay more to satisfy justice.

---

5. Psalm 89 says, "Righteousness and justice are the foundation of your throne."

The relevance of this is that the same logic applies to our spiritual lives. The more we sin, the more we increase our moral debt. This is true regardless of whether or not we sin consciously and intentionally. No policeman will listen to the excuses, "I didn't know the speed limit!" or "I wasn't paying attention to the speedometer!" To sit behind the wheel is to be accountable for one's driving. Similarly, God will not countenance the excuse, "I didn't know what I was doing!." Reason, free will, and conscience are like the speedometer of the soul. God's answer to anyone who claims, "I didn't know what I was doing!" will be the simple retort: *you should have.*[6]

Still, there is more that we can learn from the illustration.

Let's add a few details to change the significance of the speeding violations. Imagine, for example, that Steve's speeding did not occur exclusively on highways, but through school zones, construction areas, and private residences. Undoubtedly, this would aggravate the seriousness of each offense. Imagine as well that there were periodic citations and notices coming through Steve's mail, but that all of these were ignored – thus further compounding the sanctions. Imagine, too, that the speeding occurred under a foreign jurisdiction. Whereas in Steve's home country, speeding was a minor offense subject to a low threshold of punishment, under different laws this behavior was counted a severe crime. Punitive damages included not just financial penalties or suspended licenses, but jail time, even corporal punishment. Finally, imagine that the charges were not limited to speeding violations. Unbeknownst to Steve, cameras had caught multiple instances of recklessness that had resulted in bystanders being injured and properties being destroyed.

---

6. Many Western legal codes operate on the principle "*ignorantia juris non excusat.*" (Ignorance is no excuse.)

With all of this in mind, try to imagine what it would be like for Steve to finally come to terms with his actions. Picture him standing before a judge with indisputable evidence pointing toward conviction and punishment. Think about the burden of guilt that Steve would feel as he contemplates for the first time what it will take for justice to be satisfied. Reflect on the despair that would settle into Steve's heart as one-by-one all of his proffered excuses were discredited.

All of this gets us to the verge of understanding the guilt we face for sin. I say "verge" for a reason: the analogy of speeding does not come anywhere near to communicating the consequences of sin. From beginning to end, the Bible is clear that the wages of sin is death. By "death," something more is meant than a mere end to biological life. "Death," when used in connection to sin, always refers to something far worse, namely, separation from God, which is to say, separation from the source of joy, peace, light, life, and happiness. This is why sin and hell are so closely connected. Hell is the punishment that eternally pays off the debt of sin.[7]

And yet there is more to learn from the illustration.

Keep the scene rolling in your mind. Imagine, having reached a state of complete moral sobriety, that Steve falls on his knees and shamelessly begs the judge for a pardon. Now, ask yourself a question, Would it be just in this instance for the judge to grant forgiveness? If one is unbiased, the answer is *no*. To sweep aside the guilt of Steve would be an egregious violation of justice on multiple counts: it would set a terrible precedent for other drivers; it would degrade the sanctity of the rule of law; it would scorn the claims of innocent victims; and, most importantly of all, it would trample on justice

---

7. Jesus speaks more about spiritual death than anyone in the New Testament. He consistently warns of outer darkness, a place of weeping and gnashing of teeth.

itself, the abiding principle behind all fair play. For these reasons, the only just decision for the judge to make would be, "Guilty as charged." Punishment would be the clear way for the scales of justice to tilt back into balance.

Yet, all of this admitted, there is one feasible condition on which the judge could pardon Steve. This is where the logic of sacrifice intersects with the logic of justice. In order to grasp how this might be the case, we need to develop the story one last time.

Picture that, after Steve hears the verdict "guilty as charged," a stranger stands up in the courtroom and volunteers to undertake Steve's punishment in his stead. The man offers, in other words, to pay off all of the financial penalties, to serve the specified jail time, and to suffer any other prescribed punishments. Unlike Steve, this stranger has a clean driving record. This means that he can stand in as a substitute because there are no penal claims against him.

If this happened, the judge would have a choice. He could either make Steve pay for his own crimes, or he could allow the stranger to suffer the punishment vicariously. If the judge permitted the latter option, something surprising would suddenly be made possible: mercy could be offered to Steve without conflicting with justice. The judge could release Steve – not because justice was ignored – but because a pardon was purchased. Through sacrifice, justice could be satisfied without Steve himself suffering any punishment.

Only now are we ready to talk explicitly about the cross. The cross is the extraordinary instrument by which Jesus offers Himself as a substitute in the place of sinners. Because of the unique value of His person, being both the Son of God and a perfectly righteous man, Jesus was able to pay off a debt of sin that otherwise could only be satisfied through a neverending spiritual death.[8] This is the light in which we need to read the gospel accounts of the crucifixion. Throughout these narratives, we need to appreciate that Jesus is offering Himself as a sacrifice on behalf of sinners. When we hear Jesus cry out "My God, my God, why have you forsaken me?" we need to recognize the voice of a substitute freely undertaking the punishment of a guilt-ridden people. Likewise, when we hear the cry "It is finished!" we need to register the victory of a savior who has just paid off the last farthing of justice so that the guilty might go free.[9]

It needs to be made clear that Jesus can offer Himself in the place of sinners only because His moral record is completely clean. If Jesus Himself were a sinner, His own moral debt would prohibit Him from being able to stand in as a sacrifice for others. He would need to suffer punishment alongside the rest of us. But, marvelously, this is not the case. Spotless of moral guilt, Jesus is qualified to stand in for others.[10]

It must also be made clear that, because Jesus is guiltless, the Father can receive Jesus as a substitute for sinners without undermining the integrity of the moral order. Only because of the cross, can the Father justify sinners without lowering the standard of justice. Because Jesus discharged the debt of sin, sinners can go free without any protest that God is anything other than perfectly righteous.[11]

---

8. For a classic treatment of the satisfaction of divine justice see Anselm's *Cur Deus Homo* (Lulu.com, 2008).

9. To explore the intersection of justice, sacrifice, and atonement in further detail see William Lane Craig's *Atonement and the Death of Christ* (Baylor University Press, 2020).

10. Men wanting to think more deeply on the cross should read John Stott's *The Cross of Christ* (IVP, 2021).

11. Paul says that divine wisdom planned salvation so that "[God] might be just and the justifier of the one who has faith in Jesus" (Rom. 3:26).

Holiness Must Be Glorified

A lot of pastors and theologians would want to stop here. We in the West are still relatively comfortable with the concept of justice. However, as was mentioned earlier, justice is not identical to holiness. And if we want to appreciate the awesomeness of the cross, we need to move beyond the realm of justice into the realm of religion, which is to say, of holiness.

There is no way to understand holiness without ritual. More specifically, there is no way to understand holiness without the rituals that God gave the Israelites under the ministry of Moses. This liturgical code is a user-manual for interaction with God. It reveals aspects of our existence that cannot be known by any other source – at least not with equal clarity and pertinence.

Much could be said about this code. Comments here need to be limited to the bare essentials.

First, from these rituals we learn that the presence of holiness changes the moral ecosystem that we inhabit. In the space of holiness, sin is not just a trespass, a breaking of a rule; it is a pollutant, the invasion of an anti-God substance into the realm of God Himself.[12] The implications of this need to be understood. Sin is the greatest of all existential dangers. To sin is nothing less than to declare war on God. It is to conceive and bring to birth a thought, attitude, word, or deed that is contradictory to God himself. If the goal of creation is to put God's glory on display, sin is the vilification, belittling, and mocking of God. Sin is the hope that God might wither and die so that something else might fill His place.[13]

---

12. Jacob Milgrom makes this clear in his multiple commentaries on Leviticus.

13. Donald Macleod is helpful on the concept of sin as lawlessness. See *A Faith to Live By* (Mentor, 1998).

THE ROAD BACK TO GOD

Second, from the rituals of Israel we discover that, in the face of such aggression, God reacts in one of two ways. The first possibility is wrath.[14] Such vehement anger is a by-product of an intense love in the Divine Nature for all that is good, just, noble, clean, and beautiful. It's important to recognize that there is nothing deplorable about God expressing His wrath. In destroying a source of sin, God is doing two excellent things at once: He is magnifying His goodness while also removing a source of defilement that would otherwise corrupt the healthy and pristine. An outpouring of God's wrath is no more regrettable than the removal of a tumor by a surgeon. In both cases, something painful happens wholly for the sake of preserving happiness.

But there is a second way God can react to sin. This is by accepting a sacrifice. Through the shedding and application of blood two things happen: one is that the defilement of sin can be cleansed; the other is that God's holy wrath can be absorbed and appeased by a vicarious substitute.

There is much mystery in terms of why sacrifice works. The most important thing to keep in mind while pondering sacrifice is not *why* it works but *that* it works. Modern men need to appreciate that the religious guilt of sin is a terrifying reality. To step into the presence of holiness with the dirt of sin on one's hands is every bit as dangerous as stepping into a fire having been drenched in gasoline. The image is not intended to be macabre; it is meant to be honest. God's eyes are too pure to behold evil. What this means is that He can no more tolerate the heinousness of sin than flames can tolerate petrol fumes. This, in part, is why Hell exists. God's holiness will be glorified either by celebrating goodness or

---

14. John Stott defines wrath as "[God's] steady, unrelenting, unremitting, uncompromising antagonism to evil in all its forms and manifestations." See *The Cross of Christ*.

by destroying evil. There is no third way. When the dust of history settles, God will be all-in-all, which is to say that everything in existence will bring glory to Him, one way or another. From then on, sin will have no place to hide in peace. Sources of evil will either have been reconciled to God, or they will be exiled to "the outer darkness" where the just deserts of lawlessness will be put permanently on display.

We need this background to understand the cross. The cross is the place where Jesus becomes sin on behalf of sinners. In other words, Jesus contracts within Himself the religious guilt of sinners so that the wrath of God is deflected onto His own person. As the blood of Jesus is poured out, two things happen. One is that the pollution of sin is removed. The technical term for this is expiation. Through the sprinkling of Christ's blood, the defilement of sin is rinsed clean. But, secondly, God Himself is propitiated. Again this is a technical term. It signifies that the wrath of God is appeased. God needed to vindicate His name by expressing publicly His hatred of evil. He did this on the cross. The marvel of the death of Jesus is that, through the instrument of the cross, God Himself absorbed His own wrath through the person of His Son. He deflected the fire onto the God-man so that the flames would not touch anyone willing to take refuge under the rock of His mercy.[15]

In this way, the cross is simultaneously a demonstration of both wrath and grace. God's greatest display of holy anger is also His greatest display of holy love. Only at the cross do we find a way to reconcile God's intolerance of sin with His gracious desire to cohabit with sinners. Only through the cross can fear and shame be overcome so that,

---

15. Donald Macleod's short book *From Glory to Golgotha* is exceedingly useful for making sense of the life and death of Jesus (Christian Focus, 2020).

instead of shrinking back from God in terror, we instead have confidence to speak to Him as a loving Father who protects His children from the greatest sources of harm and destruction.[16]

That last point is worth sitting on and thinking more about. Throughout history it is a common feature among indigenous religions to build temples to mark out sacred space. It is not unusual for there to be, in the innermost space of a temple, a most holy site in which the idol, or image, of a god is stored. Religions use this architecture in order to communicate the point, "Here is the truth! If you want to see the hidden source of power, look here!" Christianity is unusual in that, in the effort to lead people toward the truth about God, it does not summon them to look behind the curtain of a temple. Rather, it tells them to go out on a hill and gaze upon the mutilated form of a publicly executed man. The whole of the Scriptures is like the finger of a clear-sighted prophet pointing to the bleeding form of Christ and saying, "Here is the truth! If you want to see God, look here!" The testimony of the Bible is that God was born in the form of man to do for man what man could never do for himself. In Jesus, God satisfied justice and glorified holiness, and He did all of it so that a free offer of pardon and grace could be offered to sinners, no matter how vile or depraved.

If you not only understand this message but appreciate it, seeing the personal relevance of it, there is only one response to the cross: incalculable gratitude. That God would become a man in order to die in the place of sinners is the most extraordinary act of sacrifice in the history of

---

16. Holy love is a topic worth contemplating in depth. It's hard for the Western mind to understand how holiness and love can, not just be reconciled, but be ultimately the same. P.T. Forsyth is the best guide to the topic.

the world. As sacred as the beaches of Normandy are with the immeasurable blood poured out on their sands, not even that ground is as sacred as the place where Jesus died. On the cross, God did the unthinkable. He died in the place of people who merited nothing but His just displeasure. And He did it not reluctantly, but in fulfillment of a love that had existed eternally.

Earlier we said that countless people have experienced a power through Jesus that cannot be replicated elsewhere. It was not then the time to specify what this power was. We can now give the answer. An old hymn says, "Burdens are lifted at Calvary." So it is. The cross is able to remove the burdens of shame and guilt unlike anything else. To see what Jesus has done with believing eyes is to feel the filth of shame rinsed off the soul, the weight of guilt lifted from the heart, and the terror of God replaced by a spirit of sacred devotion. It is to have an empty heart filled with love and a depressed spirit raised with joy. It is to know the holiness of God, not as a cause of dread, but as a cause of adoration and wonder. It is to have eternal life well up from within and to see the world with all of the amazement of having been born again.

Yet, we need to be careful not to get ahead of ourselves. We do not yet have enough truth on the table to talk explicitly about what it means to become a Christian. As important as the cross is, it is incomplete without the resurrection. Therefore, the next stage of this journey is to consider what it means that the God-man who died is dead no longer.

Resurrect Your Worldview

Progress has been made. The cross provides a solution for the problem of sin. We might think that now is the time for trumpets to be blasted and confetti cannons to fire as we dust ourselves off and saunter out of the cave into the freedom of the crystal light of the upper realm. Finally, breathing a sigh of relief, we can switch the perspective back from Jesus to the self, and we can pick up the itinerary of spiritual growth that seems to have stalled over the last couple of chapters. But, we need to restrain ourselves. We're not yet finished framing our understanding of the person and work of Jesus. We are not ready to rethink the predicament of the cave until we have joined the resurrection to the truths of the incarnation and crucifixion. Hence, the next rule of spiritual development is reaching clear and distinct ideas about the most remarkable event in human history: the day on which a dead man achieved immortality and leapt forth like a stag out of a gray and somber tomb.

Now, it's important to say that no effort will be made here to defend the historicity of the resurrection. You may think this is a bit of a cop out. It's not. In each generation there is at least one cynical journalist who goes out looking to disprove Christianity only to scrutinize the evidence for the resurrection and to come back as a fervent apostle of the faith.[1] These reports are fun reading. And, if such conversion narratives are insufficient for a skeptical mind, there are also scholarly books that exhaustively tackle the frequently asked questions.[2] All of this spade-work has been done more than once and need not be repeated here. Our interest is in two other questions: (a) why did the resurrection need to happen? and (b) what are the implications of the resurrection for guys inhabiting the modern world?

Why Did the Resurrection Need to Happen?

The resurrection is an anomaly; it deviates from the normal pattern of human life. Although the Bible records a handful of stories of dead people being raised back to life (Lazarus being the most famous incident), there is only one example of resurrection: the translation of embodied human life from a state of mortality to immortality. Jesus did not die so that He could live a bit longer and then die again at a riper age. To use a theological word, He was *glorified* so that He would never taste death again. His life reached a condition of being imperishable, incorruptible, and impervious to decay. Such an event is unique in human history. There is no precedent for it, and it has not yet been repeated. In this sense, the resurrection is as singular as the day on which the universe burst forth *ex nihilo*. Creation and resurrection stand together as the two greatest works of God in terms of demonstrating unbounded power.

---

1. Lee Strobel is one example of this.

2. Those looking for a long read, see *The Resurrection of the Son of God* by Tom Wright (SPCK Publishing, 2017). Those looking for a shorter read, see *Surprised by Hope*, also by Tom (N.T.) Wright (SPCK Publishing, 2011)

The strangeness of the resurrection ought to excite wonder and amazement in us. How often is it that some inane advertisement captures our attention when it promises a fix to a nagging problem like recurring debt or throbbing pain? We pause to listen because we are aware of a genuine need and are hopeful of a possible solution. Now, what problem is greater than the inevitability of death? How much energy do we feverishly expend trying to construct a sandcastle that, we hope, might keep the tide of time from washing away our name for at least a decade or two? Given this ineradicable interest in self-preservation, the gospel ought to be the *most interesting* message any of us has ever heard, because only the resurrection reports that self-existence *in bodily form* has the potential to endure as long as God Himself. If you are dismayed by the thought of death, this possibility ought to rivet your attention. The fact that one man resurrected swings open a door of possibility that otherwise is sealed tightly shut. The resurrection says that there is the chance that *you yourself* might be resurrected in a form similar to Jesus. Who could catch wind of such a rumor and not be fascinated by the prospect?

Now, we need to stick to the trail of our inquiry. The first question we were asking is this: why did the resurrection happen? Dead men don't revive due to a glitch in the mechanics of the universe. Jesus may be an anomaly, but He is not an accident. His resurrection was intentional, which is to say that it served a particular, predetermined purpose. God was signaling something when the corpse of Jesus opened its eyes and awakened to a startlingly new quality of existence. Some of the meaning of this amazing event can be appreciated if we break it down into the following points.

The Sacrifice for Sin Was Accepted

Death is not the ineluctable end of life. Death, for human beings, is the consequence of a broken covenant, which is to say, a curse. Man dies as a punishment for sin. This is why Paul speaks of death as "the wages of sin" (Rom. 6:23). The testimony of the Bible is that the tragic form of human life is not the result of an impersonal process like evolution; it's the result of a just punishment being exacted due to moral failure.

Now, we've already seen the way in which the death of Jesus is a vicarious sacrifice to satisfy justice and to appease holiness. At the cross, Jesus hung in the place of sinners so that He could suffer in His own person the penalty for their sin. *That* Jesus did this has already been demonstrated. What has not yet been proven is that the payment was accepted. The great evidence that Jesus' sacrifice was successful is the resurrection. He exits the tomb for a reason, namely, death no longer has a claim on Him. The logic of this is not hard to follow. If death is the punishment for sin, death only has a right over the body for as long as is needed to satisfy justice. Once the scales of justice are put back into balance, the guilty subject is free to live again.

This is precisely what happened with Jesus. He resurrects because the cross was viewed as an acceptable payment for the sins shouldered by Jesus at His death. Thus, it is entirely appropriate to view the resurrection as a kind of receipt for a payment received. Jesus will never need to die again because never again will He find Himself indebted to justice. Having redeemed His people from their guilt, all of it, both He and they are now free to live forevermore.

In this sense, Jesus' resurrection is a kind of proclamation of spiritual emancipation. The fact that He lives, having died, is proof to all of His followers that they do not need to fear death, sin, or the devil. None of these factors are able to separate them from the love of God. Regardless of what suffering they may experience in this life, they can be assured that the verdict on their lives is "not guilty." Paul makes this point memorably when, midway through his letter to the Romans, he declares, "There is therefore now no condemnation to those who are in Christ Jesus." In Paul's mind, a Christian cannot be declared guilty for his sin – now or at any time. The proof of this is the living Christ who bears in His resurrected body the marks of having stood in the place of guilty sinners.

There is one implication of this wonderful truth that needs to be made plain. Much of human religion is nothing more than an elaborate scheme to work ourselves out of a moral debt. Either through ritual or through self-denial, people have concocted lots of clever methods (though often painful and dehumanizing) by which they hope to cleanse themselves from the guilt of sin. The cross renders all such innovations pointless. There is only one effective way to rid ourselves of the debt of sin. It is by trusting in Jesus. Nothing more is needed; nothing more is valid; nothing more (or less) is accepted. It is simply by being brought into union with Jesus that we discover His death to be *our* death and His resurrection to be *our* resurrection.

The Blessings of Righteousness Have Been Purchased

Jesus lived a perfect life. This means that He not only avoided any of the defilement of sin; He also kept perfectly all the commandments of God. This latter point highlights a positive significance to the obedience of Christ that you may never have thought about. We can illustrate this using a mini parable.

Picture a man who is permitted to live in a nice house for a probationary period of time. If he keeps to the rules of the landlord, the house will become a permanent home. If he breaks the rules, he will be evicted. Day one of his tenancy, the man disobeys and ends up homeless.

Now picture a friend of both the landlord and the tenant showing up on the scene. He offers not just to repair whatever damages were caused by the tenant; he also offers to purchase the home of his own resources so that the tenant can have a permanent place to live. The landlord agrees and the transaction is completed. The final result is that the homeless tenant ends up being granted an enduring inheritance. This came about, not because of anything done by the tenant himself; it is completely a product of generosity and kindness (i.e., of grace). There is one more detail to note: in the future, the tenant will not live alone. The deal has been worked out such that the tenant and his friend will live together in a shared abode.

This parable should help us understand what Jesus accomplished through His death and resurrection. It's not just that Jesus canceled the negative deficit of sin; He also purchased a blessing for His people. He did this through His perfect righteousness. Throughout the Bible we see that there are not just penalties attached to sin; there are also rewards attached to obedience. All of these rewards point ultimately toward a happy condition in which God and man can dwell together without the lurking shadows of suffering and death. It's this condition that the Bible labels "eternal life."

A key aspect of the significance of the resurrection is that it is a receipt, not just that a debt has been paid, but that an inheritance has been purchased. The resurrection is evidence that finally a Savior has been found who can bring into effect all of the great blessings of God that hitherto had eluded mankind. Here it is helpful to contrast the work of the first Adam with the work of the last Adam (Jesus). Whereas the disobedience of the one led to a great fall, the obedience of the other led to an even greater restoration. In Christ, there is now hope, not just of avoiding death, but of inheriting a quality of life that is as distant from our present experience as an oak tree is distant from an acorn. The promise of the resurrection is that we, too, can one day be resurrected in the likeness of Jesus and go on to share an eternity of joy and peace in the presence of God.[3]

Eternal Life Is Embodied Life

For a number of different reasons, people in the West have often imagined eternal life in terms of "heaven." Typically, this is pictured to be a disembodied state in which people have a ghostlike existence. To be honest, in most cases little effort is expended imagining such a state for one main reason: it's unintelligible. Human beings only know what it's like to exist in a physical world with physical bodies. The idea of being pure spirit is no more imaginable to us than is the idea of being pure energy or pure light.

Now, the resurrection of Jesus contradicts this traditional understanding of the Christian afterlife. If we define our hope by Jesus' own experience, we discover that God's final plan of salvation is not to undress human beings of their bodies, but to reclothe them with something better that is imperishable and undecaying. The hope of a Christian, in other words, is to be resurrected in the likeness of Christ. This means having bodies that are not just able to interact with a physical world, but, in fact, that need a physical world in order to live, move, and have their being.

---

3. Paul's central exploration of this truth can be found in I Corinthians 15.

Anyone thinking deeply about this truth will immediately bump up against a question. Decay is not just a function of the human body; it is a function of the world around us, even of the universe itself. To contemplate the resurrection, therefore, we must imagine, not just new bodies, but a new physical reality encompassing our bodies. We need, in other words, a new heavens and a new earth.

This is precisely the hope of the gospel. Jesus' resurrection is not merely a signal of hope for humanity as a species, as if God's care for us is detached from any wider concern for His creation. Rather, the resurrection is a statement that the whole of creation will be remade so that God's glory can one day shine resplendently without shadow in a liberated cosmos.

You may think this sounds both strange and implausible. The implausibility is easy to overcome. All you need to do is unshackle yourself of a shrunken understanding of God and you will eventually discover the significance of what it means that God is creator. A creator God, as the Psalmist says, can do as He likes. This means that He can curse a universe such that it deteriorates with entropy or He can bless a universe so that it emerges like a rose from a thorn. His power is only restricted by His wisdom and His love.

In terms of strangeness, this can be overcome by a diligent and careful reading of the Bible. If you set out to read the New Testament looking for its own teaching on the afterlife you will be surprised by what you find – and by what you don't. You will discover that the resurrection is just as fundamental to the faith of Christians as is the crucifixion. The horizon of hope in the Bible is as wide and far-reaching as the universe itself. The Apostle Paul makes this point memorably when he says, "For we know that the whole creation has been groaning together in the pains of childbirth until now" (Rom. 8:22). Paul's point is that the resurrection of Jesus has kick-started a process that will only be complete when God delivers a new cosmos from the thralls of suffering like a baby from the womb. On that day, human beings will not just be standing in new bodies; they will be looking out on a brand new world ready to be tilled, explored, and enjoyed.

Jesus Is King

The resurrection, in one sense, was not a surprise. Jewish people in Jesus' day were expecting a general resurrection. They looked forward to a day when the righteous would be raised from the dead and given an inheritance in the age to come. The event that no one was expecting (Jesus' disciples included) was that one man would be resurrected first in anticipation of a subsequent general resurrection. That was a revelation that only Jesus foresaw. He was the only rabbi who was speaking of such a two-stage process to His inner circle of disciples.

That Jesus was correct in His understanding was proven by His resurrection. The question we need to ask here is this: why did Jesus need to be resurrected first? What is the point of one man conquering death in advance of a later resurrection that will one day affect all of us?[4]

Paul is the great theologian who provides the answer to the riddle. Paul's teaching is that Jesus was raised first because He was (and is) first in importance. The resurrection of Jesus is not just statement of general hope; it's the affirmation of a unique identity with a unique prerogative. In a famous speech to a group of skeptics in Athens, Paul says,

> The times of ignorance God overlooked, but now he commands all people everywhere to repent, because

---

4. Tom Wright helpfully explores this in *How God Became King: Getting to the Heart of the Gospels* (SPCK, 2012).

> he has fixed a day on which he will judge the world in righteousness by a man whom he has appointed; and of this he has given assurance to all by raising him from the dead. (Acts 17:30-31)

There are a couple of things worth noting in this quotation. The first is that God will restore justice to the world through His Son, Jesus. This is a point that Jesus Himself is diligent to make. Tying together many threads from the Old Testament, Jesus says of Himself,

> And he has given him authority to execute judgment, because he is the Son of God. Do not marvel at this, for an hour is coming when all who are in the tombs will hear his voice and come out, those who have done good to the resurrection of life, and those who have done evil to the resurrection of judgment. (John 5:27-29)

Here and elsewhere Jesus is exceedingly candid in indicating that He Himself is the appointed king who will ultimately carry a sword in one hand and the scales of justice in the other. The great proof that this is indeed the case is Jesus' solitary resurrection from the dead. His unique exit from the tomb is a signal of specialness. Jesus is the king whose judgment will determine the eternal fate of every human soul.

The other thing to note from Paul's speech is that the resurrection of Jesus indicates a season of opportunity for sinners. Paul's precise language is that God now "commands all people everywhere to repent." The idea is that there are two ways to be reconciled to God's righteousness through the lordship of Christ. One is to repent now and, in doing so, to receive a free pardon for sins committed. This is the path of faith, that is, of submitting one's life to Christ. The other is to ignore the generosity of a free pardon and, consequently, to face a later tribunal at which time the judgment of Christ will be based on the strict merits and demerits of an individual life. Either on the basis of grace or on the basis of works, every human being will be held accountable to God. This, too, is part of the significance of Jesus' resurrection from the dead.

So What Does All of This Mean for Guys in the Modern World?

The resurrection is something that flips the script of the entire structure of the spiritual itinerary that has been outlined in this book. Thus far, this book has been constructed with the framework of men being trapped in a cave and needing to find a way to exit from it. We've pictured an upper realm of life, light, and freedom and a lower realm of death, darkness, and bondage. Sin has been presented as a barrier that blocks our way of escape from an existence defined by guilt, frustration, and despair. In short, we have looked for a means of ascent that will lead us ever closer to truth and to happiness.

The resurrection is a summons to trade in this framework for something better. The resurrection tells us that we cannot patch the freshness of Christianity onto the shrunken form of a secular worldview, a classical philosophical worldview, or even a traditional religious worldview. The whole of our existence needs to be reimagined in the light of what it means that God entered into our world as a man, died in the place of sinners, and resurrected bodily as the cornerstone of a new universe. These revelations no more fit into a modern mode of thinking than squares and circles fit into the shape of a star. The resurrection of Jesus is not just the resurrection of an individual man; it is the resurrection of a new form of life, of a new vision of hope, and of a new understanding of the self. When Christ exited the tomb, He brought into existence a perspective that could not have been imported elsewhere. It's not just that our view of the afterlife is changed; our understanding of the present life is equally altered. No longer should we look to Plato's allegory of the cave to get our bearings in the universe. Something more true and more inspiring is now available. We now have a way of imagining hope that does not just involve the mind, or the soul, but also hands and feet. Eternal life does not mean merging with universal consciousness, or universal unconsciousness, or sitting on clouds playing harps. Instead, it means gardening, running, building, and dancing. The most human of activities will not cease at death. On the contrary, their deepest fulfillment is latent like seed in the future.[5]

Another way of getting our heads around all of this is to appreciate that the resurrection, rather than being a jolting surprise, is in fact the resolution of a grand story that is contained in the Bible. Throughout the Bible, we see God attempting to provide human life with a blessing that is best imagined in terms of a home, a community, a land, a garden, and a city. The Bible never depicts the final installment of this blessing to be something set apart permanently in a heavenly realm. Rather, the hope of humankind is for a glory hitherto stored away in heaven to be released on earth. When this happens, the effect will be something like when a soaking rain falls on an arid soil. The true potential of

---

5. C.S. Lewis says, "These small and perishable bodies we now have were given to us as ponies are given to schoolboys. We must learn to manage: not that we may be free of horses altogether but that some day we may ride bare-back, confident and rejoicing, those greater mounts, those winged, shining and world-shaking horses which perhaps even now expect us with impatience, pawing and snorting in the King's stables. Not that the gallop would be of any value unless it were a gallop with the King; but how else—since He has retained His own charger—should we accompany Him?" See *Miracles* (HarperOne, 1996), 259-60.

life will finally spring forth and grow strong. Human beings will reflect the happiness of God in the joy of sinless work, leisure, community, and worship. Nothing good of the present world will be lost. Instead, with the husk removed with all corruption stripped away, the fruit of God's goodness will finally be enjoyed immeasurably and eternally, without bitterness or sorrow.

But, as mentioned, the resurrection does more than provide a first installment of the future to define our expectations. The resurrection also helps us coordinate our actions in the present age. It does this primarily in two ways.

First, the resurrection tells us that the key to gain entry into future bliss is faith in Jesus. Jesus makes this point in John's gospel when He says, "I am the door. If anyone enters by me, he will be saved, and will go in and out and find pasture" (10:9). What it means to "enter" by Jesus is to trust in Him, profess faith in His identity as the Son of God, and to submit one's life to Him as Lord and Savior. Such faith is the badge, so to speak, by which we gain access, not just to grace and mercy, but also to blessing and happiness.

But still there is more. The resurrection also tells us that our lives in the present age have an unexpected sense of purpose and mission. The best way to understand this is by picturing the church to be a spreading network of heavenly colonies on earth. What God has done in sending His Son into our world is *not* to make an exit so that we can leave the world and go and inhabit an alternative realm – as if "heaven" were a kind of space station. The gift of the Son was rather a token of God's commitment to our world. When Jesus ascended back to heaven, He did so as a king who promised to come again in glory and majesty. At this second coming, He will permanently reside among His people. For those of us living in the world, this means that there is much to do in His absence. Our calling is nothing less than to live in such a way that anticipates a kingdom that will one day fill the earth as the waters cover the sea. This is what Christians mean by living "in the name" of Jesus. Our lives are meant to reflect the lordship of Jesus on earth as it is in heaven.

Such a grand mission changes everything about our existence. No longer do we live for ourselves, and no longer do we passively reflect the better or worse values of the culture around us. Instead, taking up the New Testament, we have a fresh blueprint on which to build our lives. Our job is the immense task of figuring out what it means to reshape a lifestyle, personal relationships, and individual character on the basis of a new identity, one that is founded in the death and resurrection of Jesus.

Such a challenge makes up the great adventure of the Christian life. To be a Christian is like standing on a high peak and gazing out on a vast continent that has only just been discovered and is thus unexplored. The resurrection is the loftiest place from which we can stand and view the direction of history. Once we look at life from this privileged perspective, everything takes on new meaning. We can look back and see the victory of Jesus' death on the cross. We can look forward and see a day in which all things will be made new. From this sublime position, one big question begins to govern each day's activities: How do I live according to the knowledge that Jesus is Lord *right now* and that the ravishing joy of His kingdom is ever-approaching like a tidal wave on the horizon?

To ask this question is to grasp the significance of the resurrection.

RULE 9

Act on the Truth

A kind of alchemy should have happened in the course of reading this book. The quality of your interest in religion ought to have been transmuted. In the introduction, we used the image of a boy seeing a pretty girl across the street to depict the casualness of religious interest among modern men. This metaphor may no longer be appropriate for you. If you have been stung by the poison of sin, the light of holiness, and the nails of the cross you will no longer feel relaxed in your interest; you will be struck by something like a piercing thirst. Your attitude might be likened to that of a terminally ill patient who hears news of an unexpected treatment. Whereas a guy admiring a girl from a distance will very likely walk on without further thought, a despairing patient will obsess endlessly about a possible cure. Nothing will distract him from the prospect of restored health.

Such pining interest is the mark of a man who has understood the implications of the gospel (the news about Jesus). The gospel is a two-sided coin. On the one hand, it informs us that we are guilty and in danger of imminent spiritual death. On the other, it tells us that Jesus experienced death for sinners just like us and that, if we own Jesus as Lord, we can have our record wiped clean without any fear of future judgment. You cannot comprehend these truths and scorn them. Once understood, the possibility of grace narrows down your interest to a single, pointed question: *what must I do to be saved?*

The answer to this question is the theme of this chapter. There is nothing more cruel than telling someone about a cure without giving him clear instructions about how to access it. Our goal is to avoid such unkindness. Therefore, we will be as concrete and practical as possible in terms of paving a simple and clear path that indicates to you what it actually means *to become a Christian*. Reaching this point has been the planned destination of the entire book. All that has been said thus far has been leading you to a point of decision. We have been stripping away unhelpful assumptions about human existence and restoring old, forgotten truths so that ideas could ultimately give birth to action. The final thing that needs to be done, in terms of this book being a guide, is to specify the steps needed to close the gap between curiosity and commitment. The aim of this chapter is to eliminate all confusion so that you know precisely what Jesus meant when, turning and facing the crowd, He said, "If anyone would come after me, let him deny himself and take up his cross daily and follow me" (Luke 9:23).

This chapter will be structured around five verbs: *repent, submit, profess, attach,* and *follow*. These labels should be recognised not just as actions, but as imperatives. They are authoritative words that are meant to impact the *will* and, in consequence, prompt a step of obedience. Together, they constitute much of what Christians mean by "belief" or "faith." It's important for you to know that "to believe in Jesus" is not to say a quiet prayer that more or less leaves your life intact. A true profession of faith is an experience as radical and life-changing as being adopted into a new family. In converting to Christianity, you are not adding religion into your life like a pinch of sugar into a cup of tea, a small change that merely sweetens what is already there (comparable perhaps to adding exercise or reading to a weekly routine). Rather, you are reorienting your love, fear, and aspiration around a new center of gravity. The effect of such an event is something that ripples its way through the entirety of your character and lifestyle. Therefore, you need to think carefully before taking the step of becoming a Christian. It is something more significant than choosing a profession – or even choosing a spouse. It is nothing less than the death of an old man and the rebirth of a new one.

You Must Repent

Like a lot of religious words, repentance suffers from misunderstanding. Some people think of it in terms of penance (i.e., self-inflicted punishment for the sake of paying off a moral debt). Others think of it in terms of a polite "I'm sorry" that may or may not include a measure of sincerity. Neither understanding is correct.

Biblically, there are two primary models for thinking about repentance. One is the act of physically turning. When a person is being led by sin, he is following a path that is leading him away from God. The logic of this is simple. If sin and God are mutually opposed, they cannot be pursued simultaneously. To live by sin is to move away from God just as to walk east is to move away from the west. In this sense, we can rightly say that, prior to repenting, the entirety of a person's life is a journey away from God. Although not each and every act of such a life may be sinful, the fundamental course one is following is defined by self-rule, not God-rule.

This is why the Bible often speaks of non-believers as rebels against God, even as enemies of God. If we are not for God, then we are against Him.

Repentance, then, is the act of turning from sin to God. We might liken it to a rejection of sin, a kind of saying "no!" assertively to sin. The truth is that, left to ourselves, none of us is in control of our lives. We are not pimps, using sin for our own means. We are call-girls being hustled by evil desire. Sin is the one calling the shots and directing our choices such that we drift into ever darker waters of shame and misery. Repentance is that moment when, seeing sin for what it is, we about-turn and cry out for help. Such a movement does not in itself free us from the tyranny of sin. What it does do is humble our ego and turn us in the direction of God, which is the source of mercy and grace. Likewise, turning from sin does not mean that we never sin again. What it does mean is that we stop feeling a license to do as we please. In turning toward God, we let go of the reins of our heart. The attitude we adopt is that of a servant, even of a slave. We come to God as a beggar stripped of wealth and title. Our only plea is that of grace: "God, have mercy on me, a sinner!"

The second image for repentance is a change of mindset. Now, we could focus on any number of different perspectives that change in the course of repentance. I'll just take up one. The way we view ourselves fundamentally alters. Prior to repentance, we tend to view ourselves either as a hero or as a victim. If life is going well, and we are experiencing one wave of success after another, we tend to read our lives as an epic story with the "Big Me" cast in the chief role. If life is a torrent of grief and tears, then we change the plot to a tragedy, still keeping the self as the center of attention. Repentance is a complete revision of the narrative. In owning our sin, we come to see ourselves not as heroes and victims, but as antagonists and culprits. We perceive that the climax of human history is not the brief moment when the spotlight shines on me. Rather, all hope stands or falls on the agonizing moment when the Son of God is nailed to a plank. That event becomes the center, not just of history in general, but of my own, personal life story. There is a strange way in which I find myself involved in what amounts to both the darkest and the brightest moment in history. I come to see that Jesus died in my place and that His death is both the penalty suffered on behalf of my sin and the loving declaration that there is grace for sinners – even the chief of sinners, *me*.

The result of this new perspective is the death of pride and self-pity. A gratitude-infused-humility breaks through the sedimented layers of shame and guilt so a new love fills the soul. I turn to God – not because I have anything to offer Him, and certainly not because He owes anything to me – but simply because He has made Himself irresistibly beautiful in the dying form of Jesus.

The marvel of the cross is that it conquers the two most tenacious aspects of sin. First, it humbles our pride; second, it redirects our love. Repentance is the word that we use to label the conscious experience of being caught in a riptide of divine love that leaves the soul swimming in the vast waters of forgiveness and grace.

You Must Submit

The most natural word to use here would be "believe." Throughout the New Testament, the commands *repent* and *believe* are like salt and pepper; they are usually paired. Therefore, I need to explain my motives for substituting *submit* for *believe*.

The problem with telling guys to believe is twofold. First, in the modern world, belief is corrupted by emotion. People tend to think that belief is *felt* as much as it is *known*. For example, if you ask someone, "Do you believe in God?" he will more than likely do a gut-check. If God feels present, the answer will be "yes." If God feels non-existent, the answer will be "no." No appeal will be made to logic or testimony. Emotion will have pushed its way in as chief advisor.

Second, modern guys tend to conflate belief and certainty. We imagine belief to be an ideal state in which no doubt is intermixed. This sets the bar incredibly high for people living in a secular age in which the fumes of doubt are constantly inhaled. In a modern context, faith is always going to be a desired garden, and doubt is always going to be a prolific weed. To have a healthy faith will require diligent work. Doubts will need to be repeatedly identified and dug up. The reason for this is not any inherent weakness in the truthfulness of the gospel; it is simply a consequence of inhabiting a pluralistic environment in which "authorities" consistently belittle whatever they cannot see, measure, and touch.

This explains why I'm avoiding the word "believe." Now, I need to justify my use of "submit."

One of the frustrating barriers to faith is that a lot of guys separate reality into a spiritual realm and a secular realm. Religious stuff belongs on the spiritual side of the fence. This includes ideas about God, morality, and the soul. These ideas are felt to be as distant and detached from normal life as the stars of Alpha Centauri are from the streets of Manhattan.

In contrast, material stuff resides in the secular realm. This includes politics, economics, and social interaction. This is the stuff that really matters in the sense of having an impact on everyday existence.

Now, the sad truth is that too many guys think of the claims of Jesus as belonging to the spiritual realm. Therefore, if you ask a man the question "Do you believe in Jesus?" he processes the question as if you are asking him about something in a galaxy far, far away. The language of belief triggers a feeling of disengagement. It awakens a part of the mind that most guys prefer to leave dormant.

The word "submit" avoids all of this confusion. If I ask you "Do you submit to the truth about Jesus?" it should generate an altogether different response. The imperative slices through the intellect and lands squarely on the central nerve of the will. Human beings typically submit themselves to things that are real, pertinent, and obligatory. We are far more likely to yield ourselves to a police car that is flashing its lights than we are to an abstract system of philosophy.

It's vital for you to realize that the Christian gospel is not esoteric wisdom or abstruse advice; it is *news* in the sense of a truthful report about things that actually happened. That Jesus is Lord is not some idea that has been put forth for the benefit of consumers needing therapy. Jesus is Lord in the sense that a president sits in the Oval Office and a prime minister resides at 10 Downing Street. The resurrection declares so much. It puts Jesus forth, not as a good idea, but as a Caesar among Caesars. This means that *to believe* in Jesus is to acknowledge truth in the sense of pledging allegiance to it. No belief is authentic unless it is as much an act of homage as it is an act of credence.

The benefits of such submission are exceedingly clear in the New Testament. They include the following: a full pardon of sin, citizenship among the people of God, adoption into the divine family, a share in the inheritance of the new heavens and the new earth, and the infilling of the soul with the power and love of God, which is to say, the Holy Spirit. Therefore, in submitting to Jesus, one is not really giving up anything – at least of value. All we hand over is the pretense of independence, which is the source of measureless woe. What we get in return is nothing less than eternal life. A better deal could not be imagined, much less hoped for.

You Must Profess

All that we have said so far could be done in private. One can repent in private; one can submit in private. Not so of the next imperative. The call to *profess* swings open the curtains and drags us out into the space of other people.

To understand what it means to *profess*, you need to be aware of two aspects of modern life. One is that, in Western society, we tend to treat religion as one of the most hidden and intimate dimensions of existence. A man's religion rarely peeps out in public, except among the closest of friends. In fact, a lot of men today are much more inclined to speak openly about the topics of politics, money, even sexuality, than they are about religion. Religion makes us uncomfortable for multiple reasons. It feels awkward, out of date, and socially dangerous. Thus, like medication, we tend to leave religion for formal conversations between professionals and patients. To ask a friend about God is like inquiring about his latest prostate exam: you need to be on exceptionally close terms before crossing that line.

The second thing you need to understand is that modern life is compartmentalized. There are very few aspects of our identities that permeate the whole of our existence. Marriage, for example, does not intrude upon work; neither does work interface with religion; neither does religion touch upon leisure. Modern lives are like pies that are carved into discrete pieces and given size according to priority and demand. Some areas of life are more significant, some less; very few wind up sharing space on the same plate.

Now, the call to *profess* dismantles both of these habits of living. On the one hand, becoming a Christian is an act no less public than getting married. When two people fall in love, they undoubtedly say, "I love you!" to each other. However, this communication does not constitute a marriage. To be wedded in the eyes of the law requires a ceremony involving, at a minimum, an officiant and witnesses. It is a public act, not a private act.

Something similar is true of becoming a Christian. One of Jesus' commands to His followers is that they undergo the public ritual of baptism. This ordinance is not something that is meant to be done in private; neither is it something one can do to oneself. In almost every case, it involves an officiant (often a pastor) and witnesses (usually a congregation). There are multiple layers of meaning tucked away in the ritual. I don't want to get lost in them. The relevant point here is that belief in Jesus requires undergoing a ceremony that sets faith in public view. A believer must stand up before other Christians and shamelessly own his desire to be identified with Jesus. He should no more want to keep this a secret than a bride would want to conceal a groom from her family, friends, and colleagues. There is nothing embarrassing about being identified as a Christian. To serve the king who gave His life on behalf of sinners is to hold a banner more glorious than any other. No attachment to a sports team, political party, nation-state, company, or military branch can compare. Next to the cross, every other badge of identity is rubbish. It has no value when put on the scales beside the blood of Jesus.

The idea of professing is equally destructive of the compartmentalization of modern life. You need to know that becoming a Christian is not like joining a country club. It is not a small thing that affects a fenced off area of life.

On the contrary, being a Christian is a point of identity that sinks deeper into the soul than the roots of gender, family, culture, personality, or race. It is something like leaven that permeates the whole of your being. Nothing is left unaffected. The whole of life is repurposed and reoriented.

A helpful way of thinking about the difference following Christ makes is to compare it to citizenship. To change citizenship from one country to another is no trivial choice. A massive tract of life is affected by the decision. There are privileges and responsibilities that must be pondered. The practical domains of family and employment will be regulated; the more cultural domains of values and aspirations will be influenced. To be British is a very different mode of existence than to be German or Nigerian or Japanese. Thus, it is no exaggeration to say that the choice to take up a new citizenship will result in self-transformation. Inevitably, the new identity will exert a pressure that begins to reshape the character and lifestyle of an individual.

Now, all of this is even more true for the decision to become a Christian. To profess faith in Jesus is to transfer into a kingdom that is far more distinct from the world than the United Kingdom is distinct from South Korea or Nepal. You are taking on a new identity that involves new privileges, responsibilities, values, and aspirations. Everything in life will be affected as a consequence. Your faith in Jesus will influence how you think about fatherhood, what you do with your time, how you invest your money, even your attitude toward your body. A new question will be asked of every role and responsibility that constitutes your existence. You will now need to ask, "Jesus, how can I serve you *with this part of my life?*"

To help you feel the point even more deeply, we can shift the metaphor from citizenship to ambassadorship. To be an ambassador is a far greater responsibility than merely to be a citizen. The job of an ambassador is not to build a quiet life for oneself, but to honor and represent the dignity and values of a nation. While abroad, an ambassador can never forget his office. He is not a private citizen; he fills a public role.

So it is with the Christian. Once saved from our sins, our life is not our own. Henceforth, we serve a king and a master, and, wherever we go, we must live in such a way that brings honor to his name. This is the death knell for any compartmentalized understanding of religion.

You Must Attach

Up until now, the church has been viewed as not much more than a service provider. The only time we have mentioned it is in the context of baptism. This needs to change. You need to appreciate that the Christian life must be lived out in the context of other Christians. Church membership (as will be described below) is not optional; it's imperative.

We can begin to understand this if we take up Paul's favorite image for the church – that of a body. The metaphor is an obvious one. Human society is often an *emergent system*. The life of a community is more than the sum of its parts. There is a way in which human love and commitment can result in something more like an organism than an organization. Connected by shared purpose and values, we achieve coordinated movement. We think and act as one, not just as scattered individuals.

Although this is a general truth regarding the social behavior of human beings, it has a special application among Christians. The church is more like a body than any other human society. This is the case for several reasons.

First, the virtues that constitute a Christian life require other people to practice them. Stoics can be stoics in isolation. They can practice wisdom, courage, justice, and self-control in a shack in the woods by themselves. Not so of Christians. Most of our virtues are relational. In other words, they must be put to use in the context of community. Rather than being golfers, we are footballers; we improve and mature by interacting together, not alone. The point becomes obvious once you register the emphasis on love in the New Testament. Love is the most relational of all virtues. If the Christian life is ultimately about love being perfected and communicated, then the Christian life must be lived out among other people. Self-control only requires a *self*; love requires an *other*.

Second, the disciplines that constitute a Christian life also require community. The Christian life is a disciplined life in the sense that there are certain activities that give the church order and definition. Some of the most important of these are corporate singing, the corporate reading of Scripture, and corporate prayer. Sunday worship is not an opt-in activity among Christians. We gather to worship just as soldiers gather to drill; it's simply what we do. To pray at home, or to read the Bible alone, is a wise and healthy habit. But it's not enough. One of the chief ways Christians honor Jesus is by gathering as a congregation to worship Him. We believe that we were saved, to no small extent, in order to praise God together. This is one of the great joys we share in the present life, and it's one of things we most look forward to doing in the age to come.

Third, the mission that constitutes the Christian life requires other people. Jesus has told us to be a light in the world and to go out and make disciples. This commission is not an individual enterprise. Christians are not independent salesmen who go out and try to do as much as we can for the kingdom in isolation. The light of a bonfire is much brighter than that of a candle. So it is with the church. We are most effective in reaching the world around us when people see the brightness of faith, hope, and love lived out, not individually, but in community. Jesus was clear on this point. The night before He died He told His closest disciples, "By this all people will know that you are my disciples, if you have love for one another" (John 13:35). It's the collective presence of the Christians in the world that is the most compelling witness of Jesus' kingdom.

Finally, the grace that constitutes the Christian life often flows through other people. The entirety of the Christian life is lived by means of the love of God poured into our hearts. With Paul, each one of us can say, "It is no longer I who live, but Christ who lives in me" (Gal. 2:20). Yet, we need to be careful with this mystical truth. The presence of God in us does not mean that we are self-equipped for the Christian life. Rather, very often, the strength we need for increased vitality is mediated through other people. Paul's image of the church as a body makes this point very clearly. When Paul says that Christians are individually members of one another, he means that we are dependent on each other as muscle tissue is dependent on blood, bone, ligaments, and nerves. Just as a bicep is connected to the brain only through an interconnected assemblage of parts, the Christian is connected to Jesus in and through a congregation of people. No one gets Christ as a private chaplain. To live in communion with Jesus you must be willing to live in communion with his people.

One implication of all of this ought to be obvious. When you become a Christian, you give up your independence, not just in the sense of autonomy, but also in the sense of aloneness. No longer can you operate as an island unto yourself. Instead, you must connect to a church.[1] This attachment should not be viewed as a small garnish to life, something like a club membership. On the contrary, it ought to redefine your notion of self-fulfillment. Happiness, in the kingdom of God, is unachievable apart from a growing network of relationships. Just as Christians believe that God Himself is a current of love swirling between three persons, so we also believe our deepest fulfillment is found in a dance of giving and receiving love in a community of brothers and sisters.

You Must Follow

One of the dangers of Western Christianity is that faith is sometimes perceived to be a past event. A number of evangelical traditions make the so-called "sinner's prayer" a critical part – if not *the* critical part – of experiencing salvation. People are invited to say a short prayer of repentance and faith, and, immediately afterward, pronounced to be Christians. One of the unintended consequences of this practice is that some people walk away from such experiences thinking that the Christian life is a one-time decision like getting a tattoo. Once the deal is done, life moves on. And for a lot of people, this means going back more or less to how they were living beforehand.

You need to realize that faith in Jesus results in a whole new trajectory in life. Belief is not some highly touted landmark that one visits, takes a selfie, and then forgets. Belief is a road that you join and then follow for the duration of life.

---

1. Now, this raises an obvious question: *Which church?* Obviously, there are lots of options. My advice would be for men to look for churches that (i) have a high view of the authority of the Bible; (ii) keep the cross central in their teaching and ministry; (iii) seem earnest about spiritual growth; and (iv) uphold a spirit of meekness and love – especially among leaders.

This is why Christians have traditionally used pilgrimage as one of the central metaphors for understanding the life of faith. Once we profess trust in Jesus, the GPS coordinates of the heart are reprogrammed. The big question, *where are you going?* is answered in a new, hopeful way. Instead of death being the terminal destination of life, Jesus Himself fills that place. The whole of life is lived with the expectation of one day appearing before the judgment seat of Christ. Being ready for that moment is the great intent that governs the day-to-day choices of a believer's life.

Once this is understood, the question, *Who am I following?* also takes on new significance. Much of the challenge of the Christian life stems from the difficulty of finding a way to follow Jesus in the midst of all of the distraction and temptation of the modern world. The indispensable guide for staying on track is the teaching of the Bible. The Christian holds the Bible like a traveler holds a map. It indicates the essential information we need to know in order to avoid hidden perils and to advance ever closer toward the end goal of life with God.

Here again the church needs to be mentioned. Christians do not read the Bible alone (most importantly), but rather in community with others. This is why preaching holds such a central place in our worship services. One of the main reasons we attend Sunday gatherings is to hear a faithful reading of the Bible that includes contemporary, personal application. The intention is for Christians to walk away from such sermons feeling a bit like a pilgrim who has just received instruction about a next stage of travel. We are more equipped to face imminent challenges because we have a better understanding of what it means to know Jesus and walk beside Him through the struggles of life.

Now, after reading this chapter you may be thinking to yourself, "Who would do this? Who would undertake so formidable a calling as becoming a Christian?" The answer is anyone who appreciates what it means to be saved. There is a famous martyr of the last century who made the comment, "He is no fool who gives that which he cannot keep to gain that which he cannot lose." The statement is true, but insufficient. The Christian life is not just about giving up a lesser life in order to receive a better one. The Christian life is about escaping judgment and recovering freedom. We might adjust the remark to the following: "He is no fool who trades misery for happiness." Such is the offer that Jesus holds out to *you* right now. He says, "Give me your sin, shame, and death, and I will give you my righteousness, honor, and life."

What man would agree to such terms? The answer is anyone who understands them.

Make the Greatest Sacrifice

It's worth retracing our itinerary as we near the close of our journey. We started by asking questions to try to stall the nonconscious drift of a herd mentality. We focused on three particular questions: *where am I going? who am I following?* and *is the altar (I am serving) worthy of the sacrifice (of my life)?* The objective was to jump start your intellect, to fire up your mind in preparation of more important questions yet to come.

Next, we identified the problem of the cave, both in its intellectual sense (a truncated view of reality) and its moral sense (a flaccid will). All of this was done in the hopes of inspiring a greater earnestness to pursue truth and goodness. Casual interest is more dangerous than men realize. To reflect on goodness, or truth, as if it were just some painting in a museum, is to cheapen realities that ought to inspire existence. To yawn before goodness is just as degenerate as yawning before a drowning child. Both situations, if encountered properly, ought to trigger a movement of the soul that results in definite action.

After this, we unveiled the spiritual dimensions of the plight of modern men by introducing the moral depravity of sin and the threatening presence of divine holiness. This led us to the point of what philosophers call *aporia*, an irresolvable contradiction. We were left feeling both an urgency to pursue a higher life and a despair that such a life is impossible. For a moment, it looked as if the shadows of the cave were an Alcatraz that no man could escape. We felt a bit of the agony of Paul when he says, "Wretched man that I am! Who will deliver me from this body of death?" (Rom. 7:24).

It was at this point that we shifted our vision. Instead of being focused on the self, we turned our eyes to Jesus. In three consecutive chapters we thought about the incarnation, cross, and resurrection – how Jesus had entered our darkness on a rescue mission, how He had died as a sacrifice for sin, and how He resurrected, not to release us from the cave, but to renew the creation to the same glorious existence that He himself now enjoys. These truths had an effect not unlike when the answer to a riddle is given. Man's entire set up in the universe changes when we understand it in the light of the facts of Jesus.

Only after this hopeful horizon opened did we shift the gaze back to the self. The decision to become a Christian makes no sense without a carefully drawn backcloth explaining who Jesus is and what He has done. Christianity is not most fundamentally a set of practices; the nub of the Christian faith is belief in Jesus Himself. The previous chapter was an attempt to communicate honestly what it means to have such belief. We did so by looking at the words *repent, profess, submit, attach,* and *follow*. It's important for you to realize that the chapter was not a mere digest of information; it was an invitation. Each one of those five words is an opportunity to cross the threshold from unbelief to belief and thus from being a slave of sin to being a servant of Christ.

Now, you may have made it this far in terms of *reading*, but not in terms of *experience*. Experientially, there are a number of obstacles that can halt the progress of faith. Just as adults can be stuck in extended adolescence, spiritual pilgrims can find themselves caught in the miry pits of indifference, moral guilt, or unbelief. My suggestion to you if you feel as if your spiritual growth has stalled is to retrace your steps back to the place where you last marked progress. In other words, if unbelief is the problem, figure out specifically what you are struggling to believe and go back and reconsider the topic. Don't be bullied by your doubts; wrestle with them with the passion of a man in a brawl using the weapons of logic and evidence. If the trouble seems to be located more in the will than the intellect, reread the early chapters that were written to awaken the soul from lethargy. Treat slothfulness like the deadly sin that it is. Give no more ground to apathy than you would give to drunkenness, or gluttony, or narcissism. If dithering seems to be the problem – if you feel yourself on the edge of a decision but unable to pull the trigger – go back and gaze at the cross. Ask yourself if you want to face divine justice on the basis of your own moral track record, or if you would prefer to be given the free pardon (and inheritance) that comes from trusting in Jesus.

In short, don't be content to only partially finish the journey. One of the tragic figures in the Bible is that of Terah, Abraham's father. Terah left Ur with Abraham to travel toward the Promised Land; however, for some reason, he stopped in Haran. He pitched his tent too early and never got to see the greater blessing that God had in store for the family of Abraham. Let this be a warning for you if you are content with a mere intellectual understanding of the

Christian faith. There is no benefit in stopping short of the endzone of salvation. Ninety-nine yards is not enough to get a touchdown. To receive the joy of salvation you need to step across the line of professed belief in Jesus.

Or maybe you have moved through all of the milestones of the itinerary and reached this moment with the excitement of a man in hopeless debt having all his arrears canceled and discovering, unexpectedly, abundant resources laid away in his account. Your heart may be bouncing between joy, wonder, surprise, and gratitude. You feel like one of the explorers of old who stood perched on a mountaintop, gazing on vast continents and oceans waiting to be traversed. You will be thinking to yourself, What next? Where do I go from here?

Now, every book has its limits. This book is not intended to be a guide to the Christian life, but rather, a guide to becoming a Christian.[1] For the most part, mapping that journey is now finished. Nevertheless, by way of ending, there is one final rule that I would offer the eager traveler. It is this: *make the greatest sacrifice possible.*

Every man wants his life to count. This passion is as deep as the soul itself. It can no more be drained from the soul than a river can drain an ocean. Men can deny this passion, or sheepishly ignore it, but they cannot eliminate it. It's there like the dignity of their persons, inalienable and ever present.

This understood, you need to ask the question at the outset of your Christian life: *what counts*? How do I know if I'm storing away treasures in heaven (to use a phrase of Jesus) or flushing my life down the drain by living for the gods of the culture around me?

---

1. For an itinerary of spiritual growth, see Joe Barnard, *The Way Forward: A Roadmap of Spiritual Growth for Men in the 21st Century* (Christian Focus, 2020).

When a person learns a new game, be it a sport or a board game, one of the first questions he asks is, *What am I meant to do?* There is an obvious need to figure out the difference between winning and losing, between having points put on the board and having them taken off, between wasting a turn and using it. Such questions increase in significance as the subject matter of action increases in importance. For example, it is more important to figure out what counts in a career than what counts in a hobby; it is more important to figure out what counts in a family than what counts in a company; and it is more important to figure out what counts in life as a whole than what counts in any single activity.

It is this last point that you need to ponder. Prior to becoming a Christian, you will have happily adopted the rules of life as they were given by some authority. Either a parent, or an employer, or a circle of friends, or some other less obvious source, will have indicated to you what it means to redeem life or waste it. Such rule books need to be put aside at the point you become a Christian. From now on, life must be played according to the design of God. Henceforward, the only audience that matters is the approval of a heavenly Father.

Now, I've just said that you should make the greatest sacrifice possible. What do I mean by this?

There are three ways to measure the worth of a sacrifice. The **first** is the worth of the altar on which a gift is placed. Not every altar has equal value. To give one's life to rescue donkeys is not as noble as to give one's life to rescue trafficked children. To die on the altar of a career is a lot less significant than to lay down one's life as a loving father and a faithful husband. To spend a life in service of a country club is a lot less valuable than to spend a life in service of a country. The greatest of all altars is that of God. Just as His existence is incomparably more immense than the universe itself, so there is nothing in the universe that can compete with God in terms of weight or honor. The difference between God and anything in creation is infinitely more than the difference between a planet and a grain of sand. His glory makes the sun look like a candle; His majesty makes the grandest of mountains look like an anthill; His kingdom makes the politics of any nation look like a pantomime.

Practically, this means that if you want to maximize the value of your life then you need to live and die for the sake of God. To serve God is to serve the most sacred of altars. Whereas so much of life is dew that time quickly evaporates, the service we do unto God is a service that will be remembered as long as eternity itself. This cannot be said of anything else. It is only the things that are pleasing to the heart of God that are more durable than the earth itself.

Second, the greatness of a sacrifice is measured by the nature of the gift. Long ago, people used to bring lambs and bulls in order to offer religious worship. Some of these sacrifices only resulted in a part of the animal being put on the altar. However, in Israel, there was something called a whole burnt offering (a holocaust). In such sacrifices, the entire animal was given to God. The act expressed an attitude of wholehearted devotion. God was worthy, not just of some of the offering, but of all of it.

In Romans, Paul encourages Christians with the following words: "I appeal to you therefore, brothers, by the mercies of God, to present your bodies as a living sacrifice, holy and acceptable to God, which is your spiritual worship" (12:1). Paul is challenging us here to give the totality of ourselves to God. We are to view our bodies, and everything we do with them, as an act of worship unto God. And we are to do this in a spirit of devotion, recognizing that the God who has shown such mercy to us is worthy of nothing less than the entirety of our persons.

There are any number of Christians who try to get by with half-hearted devotion to God. They live partially for God and partially for something else. Such piecemeal obedience is wasteful. To give only one half of life to God is to leave the other half rotting in the waste bin of history. It is the degree to which we live for anything other than God that life amounts to nothing more than a pile of leaves to be blown away by time.

But the opposite principle is also true. The greatest sacrifice possible is a life lived completely unto God. The more you figure out how to serve God in each and every facet of your life, the more your life will attain a substance and worth that is imperishable. Rather than building on the work of God with wood, hay, and stubble, your life will amount to gold, silver, and precious stones (cf. 1 Cor. 3). Adjusting the words of a well-known film, we might say that your deeds will not just echo through eternity; they will adorn the kingdom of God like gilded jewels on the walls of a magnificent temple.

But, **finally**, the greatness of a sacrifice is measured, not just by the altar and the gift, but by the attitudes with which a gift is offered. Duty is a poor substitute for gratitude; reluctance is an insult to love. If you want to please God as much as possible with your life, you need to make gratitude and love the aroma of all of your service. Such motives demonstrate an appreciation of what God has done, but they do more: they equally demonstrate an appreciation of who God is. After all, who could look at the cross, and understand its meaning, without feeling a tide of gratitude surging in his heart? And who could look at Jesus Himself, seeing in Him the radiance of holy love, and not feel an uncontainable pressure to offer love in return?

Perhaps the most wonderful rendering of the deep motives of the Christian life is found in the classic hymn, "When I Survey" by Isaac Watts. The hymn-writer says,

When I survey the wondrous cross
on which the Prince of glory died,
my richest gain I count but loss,
and pour contempt on all my pride.

Forbid it, Lord, that I should boast
save in the death of Christ, my God!
All the vain things that charm me most,
I sacrifice them through his blood.

See, from his head, his hands, his feet,
sorrow and love flow mingled down.
Did e'er such love and sorrow meet,
or thorns compose so rich a crown?

Were the whole realm of nature mine,
that were a present far too small.
Love so amazing, so divine,
demands my soul, my life, my all.

You need to ponder the final two lines of the hymn. They remind us that the only just reply to the love of God seen in Jesus is a total offering of oneself to God in unconditional devotion. Anything less is an insult to grace and a rejection of beauty.

As we come to an end, I'm sure you may be grateful if I could spell out in more detail what it looks like to lay down one's life as a sacrifice on the altar of God. But, saying much more is unhelpful for two reasons.

First, the Christian life can never be reduced to a simple formula. This is due, in part, to the fact that God's interest in our lives goes beyond a limited set of activities, like saving souls and reading the Bible. The Christian life is not like

American football, in which there are only a few ways to put points on the board, mainly through touchdowns and field goals. God's interests are as manifold as are the works of creation. The truth is that there are as many ways to serve God as there are Christians in the world. No man's life is the same as another's, which is why one of the great challenges (and pleasures) of the Christian life is "to work out your salvation with fear and trembling" (Phil. 2:12). Each Christian must, in other words, figure out for himself what it means to live a good and honorable life. There is no universal script to be downloaded. There is no simple scorecard that you can pick up from your local church. Instead, you must take the blueprint of the New Testament and, using the raw material of your particular circumstances, build a temple that is worthy of the living God.

But, second, no more advice will be given due to the fact that the end of this book is, in truth, the launching point of a new journey. Once you have come to faith, you are not done traveling and ready to settle down. Rather, salvation is the point of departure for what is the greatest of all pilgrimages. This is a point that Augustine, Dante, Chaucer, and Bunyan have all made in their own way. At the point a man is saved, he is then in the position of Abraham, a sojourner on earth, awaiting a kingdom to be fully revealed. In Hebrews 11:8-10, we read:

> By faith Abraham obeyed when he was called to go out to a place that he was to receive as an inheritance. And he went out, not knowing where he was going. By faith he went to live in the land of promise, as in a foreign land, living in tents with Isaac and Jacob, heirs with him of the same promise. For he was looking forward to the city that has foundations, whose designer and builder is God.

When you come to faith, you will increasingly come to feel as if you both have a home and don't. The world around you will seem familiar and strange at the same time. So much of your life will materially be unchanged and yet, spiritually, everything will look and feel different. Like Abraham, you will be traipsing through the world, awaiting an inheritance that will only be fully given on the day of resurrection.

It will be from this position of a pilgrim that you will need to take up your Bible and, in community with other Christians, read it like a survival guide to an unknown territory. There will be no short-cuts for identifying perils and no single itinerary for getting through life safely. Instead, like the Israelites in the wilderness, you must seek daily your spiritual food and look repeatedly for spiritual guidance.

Yet, in spite of these difficulties, and inevitable failures, there is one truth that you must know in order to persevere. It is the simple principle that the Christian life is sustained by grace from start to finish. The justly famous hymn "Amazing Grace" states this truth as follows:

> Through many dangers, toils and snares
> I have already come:
> 'tis grace has brought me safe thus far,
> and grace will lead me home.

The wonder of salvation is that, when Jesus saves you, He fills you with His own Spirit. From then on, you are not limited to your own strength, but have the very might of God operating from within you. This is the basis of hope in the Christian life. The Christian is someone who can say with Paul, "I have been crucified with Christ. It is no longer I who live, but Christ who lives in me. And the life I now live in the flesh I live by faith in the Son of God, who loved me and gave himself for me" (Gal. 2:20).

There are a thousand things that could be said about the Christian life. But the most important one is this: Being a

Christian is trusting in Jesus for everything. Just as we are saved by no goodness of our own, we persevere due to no strength of our own. From beginning to end, the Christian life is Christ in us, the hope of glory.

Recognizing this should only deepen the love and gratitude we feel toward God. How amazing that the Holy God would take such interest in sinners! It defies logic. It silences reason. It reduces life to a single question: *How, Lord, can I serve you today?*

If you ask this question, you are ready to make the greatest of sacrifices. You are ready to offer your life as one big "Thank You!" to Jesus.

Recommended Resources

If you have finished the book and are looking for further guidance, here are some recommended resources:

1. Find a Local Church

No one practices football by reading books about football. Likewise, no one practices the Christian faith by reading books about the Christian faith. To explore Christianity, you need to find a church. You will learn far more from interacting with actual believers than you can glean from thinking alone in an armchair – or much worse, scrolling clickbait on YouTube.

Find a church that takes the Bible seriously, that makes much of Christ crucified, and that summons members to live joyful lives of service and obedience. Such a church will be a school, a hospital, and a gymnasium for your soul.

2. Start Following Cross Training Ministries

Cross Training is a ministry committed to helping men build a lifestyle of putting Christ first in the modern world. Their core values are simple routines, bodily discipline, and spiritual friendship. If you are looking for a path to spiritual growth, check out their resources. On their website you'll find podcasts, articles, programming, and specialised books. www.xtrainingministries.com

3. Read Strategically

Books aren't everything, but they are important. Here is some essential reading for men who are still finding their footing in the Christian faith.

First, read the Bible. Be focused in how you do this. The Bible is a vast continent. It will take years to explore the whole of its message. Therefore, be thoughtful about where you begin. The first five books every man should read are the Gospel of John, Paul's letter to the Romans, Genesis, Psalms, and Proverbs. This reading will pass quicker than you think and will be an appetizer of the inexhaustible feast that is the Bible.

Second, read John Bunyan's classic, *The Pilgrim's Progress*. If the original version is too difficult, find a copy in modern English. The book has been an invaluable guide to life for countless men. You need to be numbered among those who have downloaded its message onto your soul.

Third, read the logical sequel to this book, *The Way Forward: A Road Map of Spiritual Growth for Men in the 21st Century*. If the present book is about getting men to the point of being newborns in the Christian faith, *The Way Forward* is about growing newborns into mature men of faith and character.

Acknowledgements

Many hands have gone into the making of this book. I would like to acknowledge, first, the help given by my editor, Anne Norrie, whose insightful comments vastly improved the overall quality of the manuscript. Second, I want to give thanks for Evan McGinty whose friendship has shaped every aspect of my thinking regarding how to help men grow spiritually in the modern world. Third, my dear wife, Anna, also deserves praise for how patient she is to listen to me chat at length about whatever is on my mind. Fourth, I would like to thank Holyrood Evangelical Church for the prayer and support they give me day by day in all of the work that I do. Finally, I'm grateful for Christian Focus's willingness to trust an eager writer and to walk with me through the steps of imagining, writing, editing, and publishing books.

Also Available from Joe Barnard ...

THE WAY FORWARD

A Road Map for Spiritual Growth
for Men in the 21st Century

978-1-5271-0467-9

"... a fresh look at the obstacles and opportunities men face as they seek to be built up into the image of Christ."

—J. Garrett Kell
Pastor, Del Ray Baptist Church, Alexandria, Virginia

SURVIVING THE TRENCHES
Killing Sin Before Sin Kills You

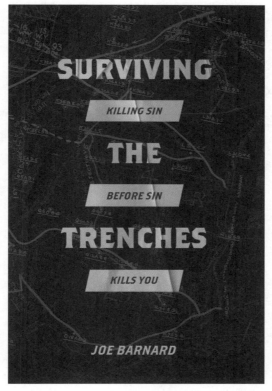

978-1-5271-0857-8

... a call to spiritual arms that should be read by every Christian.

—**Reagan Rose**
Founder, Redeeming Productivity

Christian Focus Publications

Our mission statement
Staying Faithful

In dependence upon God we seek to impact the world through literature faithful to His infallible Word, the Bible. Our aim is to ensure that the Lord Jesus Christ is presented as the only hope to obtain forgiveness of sin, live a useful life and look forward to heaven with Him.

Our Books are published in four imprints:

◁◯✕ CHRISTIAN FOCUS

Popular works including biographies, commentaries, basic doctrine and Christian living.

◁◯✕ MENTOR

Books written at a level suitable for Bible College and seminary students, pastors, and other serious readers. The imprint includes commentaries, doctrinal studies, examination of current issues and church history.

◁◯✕ CHRISTIAN HERITAGE

Books representing some of the best material from the rich heritage of the church.

◁◯✕ CF4KIDS

Children's books for quality Bible teaching and for all age groups: Sunday school curriculum, puzzle and activity books; personal and family devotional titles, biographies and inspirational stories – because you are never too young to know Jesus!

Christian Focus Publications Ltd,
Geanies House, Fearn, Ross-shire,
IV20 1TW, Scotland, United Kingdom.
www.christianfocus.com